MW01124694

HOW GOOD NONPROFIT OFFICERS BECOME GREAT

FUNDRAISERS

Implementing the 7 Powerful Strategies
To Ignite a Fundraising FIRE

BILL YOUNG

**HOW GOOD NONPROFIT OFFICERS BECOME
GREAT FUNDRAISERS**

Implementing the 7 Powerful Strategies
to Ignite a Fundraising FIRE

Copyright © 2010 Bill Young

Published through Management Factor, Inc. and Printed/
Distributed by Lightening Source/Ingram Content
Company. This book was magnificently edited by Sally
Young and the excellent interior design provided by
Karen Saunders and Kerrie Lian. Incredible cover graphic
illustration by Kerrie Lian.

This publication is meant to help your growth and
development as a Nonprofit Officer/Leader. However, it is
not a substitute for advice of your lawyers, accountant,
board of directors, government agencies, or any of your
advisors, personal or professional.

If you would like more information about webinars, training
or additional books, please visit BillYounginspires.com or
call 720.221.9214. To order more books or subscriptions
click on Bill Books on the BillYounginspires.com web site.

978-0-615-37824-4

Printed in the United States of America

This book has a companion Fundraising Fire Course in both webinar and in person formats. In order to get the most benefit from the material, we recommend you sign up for the academy to receive hands on, real world training. We all take in information differently depending on our strengths and biases.

We offer special opportunities to attend webinars throughout the year. The Directors Webinar Briefing helps you understand how your board can benefit from one of Bill's packages.

preface

THANK YOU FOR PURCHASING THIS BOOK AND FOR ATTENDING the webinar or workshop. You have thousands of choices when it comes to investing in improvement tools and I'm grateful you've chosen this one. Welcome to a new fundraising world! If you're reading this book, it means you currently are leading the fundraising efforts of a nonprofit organization (abbreviated NPO throughout the book) as either the Development Officer/Director, Executive Director, CEO, VP Development, Founder or you are a key volunteer contemplating taking the plunge to become an important internal fundraiser. Whether you are a veteran Officer or new to the field, you'll face several challenges when you perform your fundraising activities. If you don't have use a system with proper tools you'll soon become de-motivated or disgruntled and your results will not match your intentions.

I've spent many years with my fundraising hat on, watching, listening, and learning how to fundraise. In some cases I've seen what to do and how to do it well and in other cases; I've seen what not to do. As a volunteer board member I would estimate that I've spent over 5000 hours offering assistance and consultation on the topic of fundraising and read over 100 books on the subjects of both self development and fundraising.

I've been instrumental in helping raise multiple millions of dollars in both the nonprofit and for profit fundraising worlds by developing my own fundraising system. Indeed, my experience of helping strategically change the culture and fundraising levels of a very successful volunteer foundation in the Denver area was intense, leading 75 volunteers to increase their fundraising efforts each year. We experienced a new culture, implemented a different leadership style, fostered expanded team goals, and pursued new strategic commitments while raising millions of dollars for hundreds of local children's charities. Our results were dramatic when you consider we raise more funds than foundations 10 or 20 or even 50 times our size.

In addition to developing my own fundraising system, I've helped start several businesses over the last 15 years, raising angel and venture capital, connecting with strategic partners, developing sales/business development personnel and personally selling the different products and services offered through the firms. Furthermore, I've studied business intelligence and completed several training courses and workshops in entrepreneurialism. When you add in over 15 years of intense sales and marketing training, you'll understand why I'm excited and passionate about what I have to offer in this book. I've read a lot and been trained by some of the best, but the most important part of my experience is real life experience or as they say in the military "real bullets flying." In fact, I have been in the trenches using the strategies in this book to raise money through professional relationships, personal network contacts, and corporate alliances.

How A Good Nonprofit Officer becomes a Great Fundraiser is about taking small steps that lead to large impacts. In our *Fundraising Fire Course (How Good Become Great Academy)*, we teach NPO executives, development directors, board members, entrepreneurs, and internal staff to use tools and a system to improve their individual contributions. You need to concentrate on reinforcement and customized tools. The key is to learn a system that is simple and customized to each person's individual styles, preferences, and day-to-day activities; helping NPO development officers and leaders get better. The goal is not to achieve perfection, but to focus on "improvement over perfection." I've kept this saying in mind during the journey of improving both my internal thoughts and beliefs and external fundraising skills. As you read this book keep in mind that this is your chance for "improvement over perfection."

There are many books on individual development and creating effective fundraising campaigns but few focuses on the fundraising activities of individual Development Directors, Executive Officers, and key staff members. This book presents strategies in a system that is simple, customizable, and reproducible. I focus specifically on the day-to-day tasks an Officer can implement through the normal activities of their role to become a great fundraiser. One of the best ways you can help your organization thrive or survive is improve your own skills. Even if you are currently an above average fundraiser, you can get better by learning the strategies and system in this book.

Good Nonprofit Officers can Become Great Fundraisers
Great Fundraisers create Great Organizations.
Great Organizations grow and Succeed -
Start the FIRE!

About the author

A successful entrepreneur and civic leader, ready to share his expertise.

Bill sees himself as an inverse paranoid; convinced that there is a vast conspiracy to make him successful. He has spent his life studying how good become great and now wants to help as many nonprofits and entrepreneurs fulfill their fundraising goals no matter how large or small.
If you're a non-profit leader or business entrepreneur, you may share Bill Young's desire to leave a mark – by bringing revolutionary products or services to market or by improving your community.

As an entrepreneur, he has raised millions of dollars for companies in his capacity as Board member and owner. As a civic leader, he has raised millions of dollars for children's organizations throughout the Denver area. The *Denver Business Journal* named Bill to its prestigious Forty Under 40 list and recognized one of his companies, XploreNet, as the sixth Fastest Growing Privately Held Company in Colorado.

Like many successful entrepreneurs, Bill gives back to the community.

Deeply committed to improving his community and others' lives, Bill is active in leadership roles in multiple not-for-profit organizations. What motivates him? Helping kids. He believes when you help kids successfully navigate childhood, chances are they'll become responsible adults and ultimately contribute to the community.

During the past decade, Bill has applied the skills that made him a successful businessman to raise funds for nonprofits. And countless Denver children have benefited. Bill loves the feeling of being a part of something much bigger than himself. He's proud to contribute to the success of these organizations – and leave his mark on the community.

"An entrepreneur seeks out great ideas ... and may be a bit crazy."

"An entrepreneur," Bill says, "must believe so completely in an idea that you'll work around the clock to bring it to fruition. An entrepreneur looks for great ideas or people with great talent, and then finds ways to provide the vision, processes, and money to achieve success."
Bill believes such great ideas can positively impact our lives, which is why he works so hard to bring them to market. Although he readily admits some might call this crazy, he calls it satisfying.

This book is dedicated to all the amazing people who have made my life incredible. I have been very blessed and grateful for all the opportunities and interactions. The world is a better place because of these people.

My wonderful wife Karen and amazing children Ella and Braedy

My Sister Sally Young

Grandparents Francies and Harlan Gibbs

The many business partners who helped feed my entrepreneurial addiction

All the great men of Denver Active 20-30 and the many wonderful nonprofits we've been able to help over the last 23 years

The many under paid nonprofit professionals who work tirelessly each day to help those less fortunate and sacrifice to make the world a better place

Table of Contents

introduction

How Good Nonprofit Officers Become Great Fundraisers

A RECENT WALL STREET JOURNAL ARTICLE[1] POINTED OUT THAT, "The story is the same across the country. The once-booming nonprofit sector is in the midst of a shakeout, leaving many Americans without services and culling weak groups from the strong. Hit by a drop in donations and government funding in the wake of a deep recession, nonprofits— from arts councils to food banks—are undergoing a painful restructuring, including mergers, acquisitions, collaborations, cutbacks and closings." In fact, the winds of change and pressures never before seen are in full force with regard to nonprofit fundraising. Before the recession, charitable giving had increased dramatically to a level near $300 Billion in the US in 2006, however difficult and uncertain

---

[1] Robert A. Guth, Wall Street Online 2010

times have caused decreases in giving. In fact, according to American Public Media[2], most large charities are expecting a 9% decrease for 2009 and double digit decreases for 2010. This current challenge is exacerbated by the fact that [3]Boardsource (National nonprofit association) data reflects that 95% of nonprofits report that fundraising is still their number one issue.

Almost a battle-like atmosphere has been established which includes people from different political perspectives, small and large businesses and communities attempting to reduce the amount of funding for nonprofit organizations (NPOs) and in some cases, change the way they are taxed or structured. On the other side, stand the NPO leaders attempting to stay in business, grow, and thrive while overcoming the constant pressure caused by the reduction in the amount of funding from government sources and the reality of large cuts to government budgets such as Medicare. Nonprofit Officers must become exceptional fundraisers and continue to diversify their streams of revenue, avoiding the devastation that occurs when the sole source disappears.

Rest assured that the majority of society still appreciates, approves of, and helps the less fortunate and those who make sacrifices to help those in need. In fact, the green movement, spiritual awaking, and concern over natural resources further demonstrate that society wants to help, but the issue of shifting costs takes center stage when talking about the survival and eventual growth of nonprofits. As an officer of an NPO, whether the organization is a religious group, membership based, trade association, or focused on helping children or the elderly, you have a critical role in deciding whether or not the organization sur-

---

[2] American Public Media Interview 2009)
[3] BoardSource Report 2007, National Center for Nonprofit Boards

vives the next 24 to 48 months with your own fundraising activities reshaping and ultimately pushing the organization's mission forward. In order to address cost shifting, you must focus on the donations, sponsorships and in-kind trade (Power Partners) that come in via your day-to-day prospecting activities, fundraising behavior, and individual skills. This starts with changing the words you use like calling donors, sponsors, and contributors investors and ends with finding, starting, improving, growing, and maturing all your key relationships.

Solution

Development Officers, Executive Directors, Key Executives, and Internal Staff have a few options for overcoming these challenges including passively waiting for grant money, increasing board size, relying on volunteers, using traditional marketing campaigns, or utilizing a third party tool/expert. The first option is part of your revenue mix, but involves more of a "wait and see" approach while option 2, increasing board size, adds dead weight to the process by increasing board size to 30, 40, and 50. In fact, most leaders are unable to get their board to fundraise and frankly lack the time and tools to keep them on track (*How Good Board Members Become Great Fundraisers* covers this topic). Using traditional marketing campaigns or empowering volunteers should be part of your overall efforts, but can lead to frustration because of the necessary required funds to keep the campaigns successful, the number of times you have to "touch" someone before they notice your organization, and the required time to implement properly designed volunteer programs.

Therefore, the best solution is option three, using a third party system, to receive hands on, and customized individualized training to improve your skills, attitude, and activity.

It's time to set your fundraising on fire and use a third party motivator or "coach" (as such), who can deliver consistent tools, motivation, and innovative ideas via webinars and an in-person training environment. This is real, customized training at the individual level that increases the number of investors (donors, sponsors, and in-kind trade) you bring to your organization.

The new reality is that everyone has to do more with less and although entities will run, hide or quit during these challenging and changing times, others will rise above the rest; raising more money than ever before while establishing new records in the process. This requires many types of changes including new attitudes, vocabulary, beliefs, and behavior.

The fundraising world is transforming at the speed of light with new challenges and new opportunities connecting, but if you don't change your habits and the culture of your organization, then you'll continue to do what you've always done. In fact, as the new attitude and movement over the next five to ten years may provide, there seem to be three different approaches to fundraising.

1. Good Officers become great fundraisers through connecting to a third party innovative training system [IDEAL]

2. Traditional NPO Leaders keep doing things the way they always have done and hope that they stay in business [TYPICAL RESPONSE]

3. Executives that are out of business (probably don't know it yet) rely on government contracts, passive activities, or someone else to figure it out for them [NOT EFFECTIVE]

NLP Officers are first and foremost Fundraisers and have three options:

1. Wait for grants/checks to come
2. Find others to write checks
3. Find resources and relationships that turn into value

You can see the challenge that appears when Officers attempt to fundraise. Many fill their day with important duties but put critical fundraising activities at the bottom of their priority list. These fundraising or prospecting activities are paramount to serving more clients and enhancing your existing programs. In fact, we can estimate that nearly 75% to 85% are uncomfortable with prospecting activities which are defined as calling and meeting potential investors (sponsors), networking with potential investors (donors), asking for referrals, and leveraging relationships to create in-kind partnerships (Power Partners).

Whether you use traditional funding processes or new cultivation models, you still need to get people into the circles, path ways, and flow charts. This process starts with changing your vocabulary and calling donors/sponsors investors and continues into your day-to-day activities. In fact, when it comes to actual day-to-day follow through, the tried and tested for-profit prospecting tactics can help you avoid many of the challenges brought on by lack of training, process, time, and focus. However, these for-profit solutions must be customized for the nonprofit world and delivered to you by someone who has lived in your environment. Furthermore, new approaches, tools and a shift in paradigms are required to counter the outdated methods.

There are too many people asking for money or inviting investors to attend events using the wrong approaches and tools. It is not about just asking for money, but rather letting the process and tools do the asking and inviting for you; customized to your time schedule, personality, and style. Both experienced and new Nonprofit Officers need new strategies to overcome the 12 challenges outlined in the first section of this book, increasing both the volume of sponsors and number of donors.

Many Officers become great leaders, but the fundraising part seems to elude them. Their passion and desire to help is second to none and with a full head of steam they press forward to make a difference, sacrificing time and resources. They provide the organization with experience, labor, and passion for serviced clients. The lack of proper knowledge and a system leaves only experience, trial and error, and personal motivation to guide them.

The reality is that great fundraisers see the past as a resource, they are committed in the now, and they are willing to tackle the future. In the end, they realize that if they do not bring their best efforts to the entity whether it is for six months, one year or five years, the entity will cease to exist. They need the seven strategies and 34 Elements (major tactics) presented later in the book to help their NPO succeed, going from good to great in the process. These strategies are built on the core pillars of the acronym FIRE.

FIRE is about propelling momentum, influencing behaviors, expanding your influence, and creating new fundraising results for the organization.

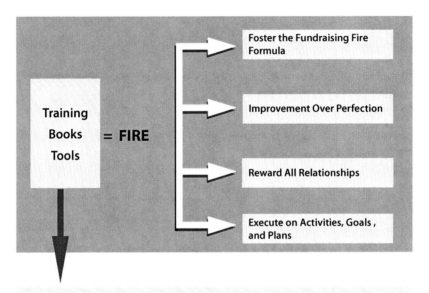

Fundraising Fire Course at the How Good Become Great Academy is an 8 week course and productive for both new Officers or helps veterans stay on target

Many of the ideas and concepts expressed in this book you've heard before however you will also learn new tactics and techniques that if implemented, will improve your efforts by 50% and in some cases 1000%. Before we get into specific tactics we'll cover the challenges briefly which are called assumptions in this book because I'm assuming you've experienced them in the past or are facing similar ones now. In fact, these challenges incapacitate many NPO Officers day-to-day fundraising efforts causing their results to fall well below expectations. For you to start "improvement over perfection", you need to understand the 12 assumed challenges and they're impact on your activities.

1: The NPO Time Trap

YOU ARE KIND, HEART-FELT, HELPFUL, CONSISTENT, IMPRESSIVE, giving, and committed. In addition, you work in the NPO world which is not known for high salaries, quarterly bonuses, or other ravishing perks, but you still give 100%. You work long hours wearing multiple hats responsible for several important aspects of the entity. One of the challenges you inevitably find yourself confronted with is too much to do and not enough time to do it, placing you smack dab in middle of the NPO time trap. You're looking for ways to increase your personal fundraising contributions, but the options must fit your professional style, enhance your other roles, help your growth, and not incapacitate your priorities and responsibilities. Your attitude and motivation often suffer in response to this situation.

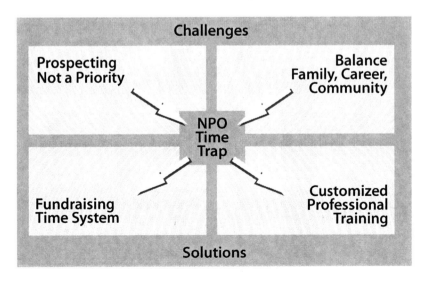

a s s u m p t i o n

2. Prepare To Prepare To Do

YOUR INTENTIONS ARE GOOD AND YOU TACKLE YOUR YEAR, MONTH, and day with vigor and zest. You organize your leads, files, computer, letters, etc., but you find yourself not working on priorities or the day ends before you can accomplish key tasks. This is being caught in the "Prepare to prepare to do" cycle or get ready to get ready. It means you spend too much time on preparing and not enough time on doing. You need to get out on the street, on the phone, in front of major prospects and try new techniques and processes. In the end you push forward often falling down when you make mistakes, but you get better via practice. You no longer prepare to prepare and instead you plan and DO.

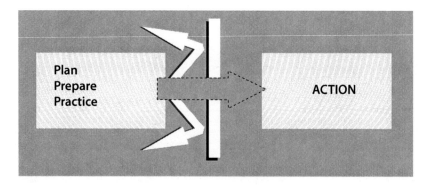

Plan
Prepare
Practice

ACTION

assumption

3: Donation Threshold Level©

YOU CONTINUE TO BRING IN THE SAME AMOUNT OF FUNDS EACH year. Your expectations are based on that amount and the skill level required to raise significantly more funds is lacking. NPO Officers become trapped by what they've accomplished up to today. Furthermore, all of your activities, relationships, and resources are based on the top number or the highest level of your current money script. You simply built your ideology around your current resource model and circle of influence. You'll need to shift your thinking in order to break through and utilize new networking tools to meet people/contacts that can bring the higher donor and sponsor value to your group and provide larger investments. This change can often mean significant increases in funding levels.

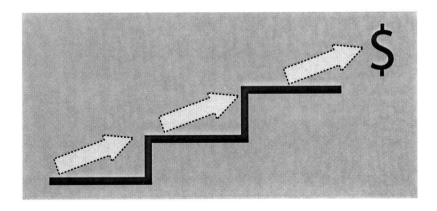

assumption

4. The Knowledge Ceiling

YOU DON'T HAVE FOR-PROFIT SALES EXPERIENCE OR IF YOU DO it is often hard to transfer those skills to the nonprofit world so your growth becomes capped. NPOs need Development Directors and other key executives to jump in and start fundraising right from the start. Their intentions are good, but their options are limited. Your knowledge about fundraising is limited so you end up caught in a cycle of either using ineffective, outdated behaviors, or failure via trial and error. In many cases you simply do nothing, caught in "analysis paralyses," or you're not sure what the next move should be. This circumstance makes you hit the ceiling very quickly. As the cycle continues, you become more frustrated often losing your motivation and in the end reducing your contribution level. You need new training.

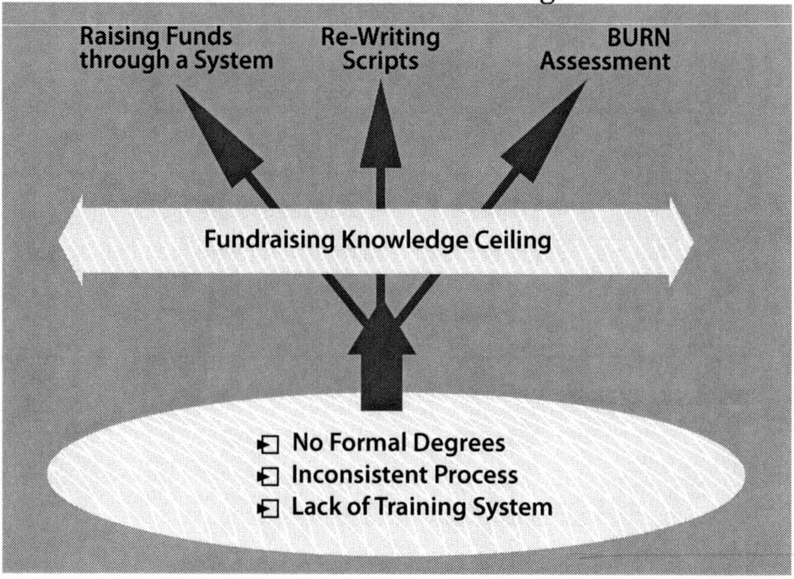

Raising Funds through a System	Re-Writing Scripts	BURN Assessment

Fundraising Knowledge Ceiling

🗲 No Formal Degrees
🗲 Inconsistent Process
🗲 Lack of Training System

assumption

5: Eagerness Trap

YOU OFTEN ASSUME WHAT THE PROSPECTIVE INVESTOR IS SAYING, suggesting, or thinking. This conversation may be taking place in your on head. In fact, you might jump to presenting solutions that don't fit the prospective investor's needs or desires because you were too eager. You find yourself in the Eagerness Trap when you don't ask the right questions at the right time to identify the real issues, preferences, and experiences of the prospect. Many prospects hide their true feelings and intentions because they've been lied to or cheated in the past. When your skeptical and allow the other person to prove to you by answering your questions in a certain way, you set the tone for the relationship and interaction.

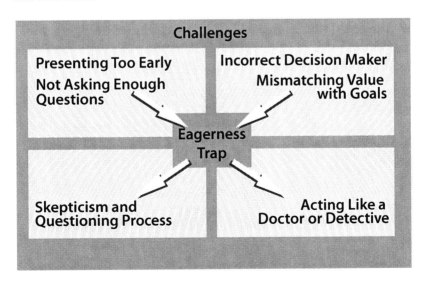

assumption

6: Negative Past Experiences

YOU HAVE EXPERIENCED THE BAD AND UGLY ESPECIALLY WHEN you watched the Board Chair uncomfortably push, probe, and unfortunately in some situations, abrasively direct the board to raise more money. You felt the pressure from not hitting goals and at times you've felt the emotional vale in the room going back and forth from the quiet of a pin drop to the brink of uncomfortable laughter, ready to explode into anger at any moment during key board and executive committee meetings. You sat there either confused and de-motivated by the process or you took the initiative and overcame these issues on your own, bringing in lots of investment (sponsors, donors, and resources). Furthermore, your negative experience was compounded when you were told to raise more funds without training or a system. This entire fundraising dance left you feeling overwhelmed and isolated. It is time to create positive feelings and activities.

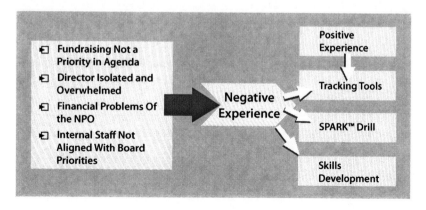

assumption

7. The Borrower Phenomenon

YOU TIGHTEN UP WHILE THINKING ABOUT ASKING OTHERS FOR money or inviting them to attend a cultivation event or asking them to send in their sponsorship agreement in because you have mental scripts playing in your head often without your conscious awareness. For some, the reluctance to invite or ask major/critical prospects is caused by weak time management skills or the lack of proper techniques, but in most cases your mental scripts are stalling your efforts from the start. These scripts deal with all kinds of categories including human interaction, ego issues, intelligence, and personal expectations, with the most well established ones surrounding money. You can use techniques and tools to improve your confidence and break through this phenomenon – doubling/tripling your results.

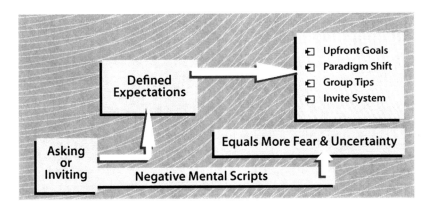

a s s u m p t i o n

8: Inefficient Personal Network

YOU ARE UNABLE TO FUNDRAISE AT THE LEVEL YOU WOULD LIKE because your existing network is not large enough, lacks strength and depth and is not expanding fast enough. Furthermore, your front line contacts have a reduction in their circle of influence or you've saturated them. You may have the misperception that everyone is getting hit up by everyone, everywhere. You could be struggling with utilizing the proper way to make a new contact or even worse you are committing one of the seven deadly sins of networking. Now add to this situation that you lack the initiative to go to new events or upon arrival the fear of creating new contacts is paralyzing. You need a new game plan for networking and increasing the right introductions and referrals.

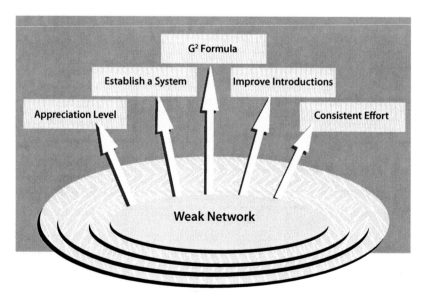

a s s u m p t i o n

9: Iceberg Phenomenon

YOU CONVEY TRUST TO OTHERS, BUT ARE THEY RESPONDING IN THE same way. Trust is a very subjective concept and felt with many different emotions from the trust you would feel with the paramedic as they take you out of a mangled car to the trust you have with your significant other. They are actually similar trust levels just ignited by different circumstances. The reality is that prospective investors protect themselves and often only tell you part of the truth, not that their lying but rather not telling the entire story. You might find that you're not asking them anything, but telling them how great your entity is or how badly you need the money. You start to look like all the other NPOs, therefore, they disengage and tell you want you want to hear or worse yet tell you nothing at all (go into hide mode). You must ask better questions at the right time and lead the investor to where they want to go.

What They Show

What They Are Really Thinking

assumption

10: The Giving Trap

YOU BECOME EXCITED AND MOTIVATED ABOUT RAISING MONEY, pouring over your contact list and outlook database identifying who to approach. You've learned new processes and techniques for expanding your network and elevating your contribution. This trap is built on great intention but marred with potential land mines. Investors gratefully give both money and time signing up their company to sponsor your event or NPO, and even donating loads cash to you. However, now the trap grabs hold of you. Reciprocal giving is a major part of the fundraising game and unless you have the budget to give to 100 or even a 1000 different organizations depending on the size of your network you'll go broke or lose your employment. You need a new strategy based on techniques that help avoid this trap, but still build confidence in your relationships.

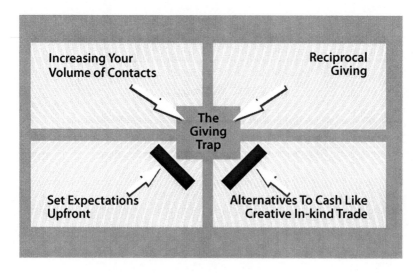

Increasing Your Volume of Contacts

Reciprocal Giving

The Giving Trap

Set Expectations Upfront

Alternatives To Cash Like Creative In-kind Trade

assumption

II: Lone Wolf Phase

YOU START EACH DAY, EACH STAFF MEETING, AND EACH BOARD meeting off with an uncomfortable feeling in your stomach. It isn't the dinner you had last night, but rather the lack of confidence you have in your fundraising system (if you have one). You've forgotten the power of other people's efforts and you're struggling through the process with one hand tied behind your back. There are new, innovative ways to approach fundraising sources and potential major investors, but you're still using outdated tools. It's time to create SuperStars and avoid facing your future fundraising goals alone. The help you need is an arm's length away.

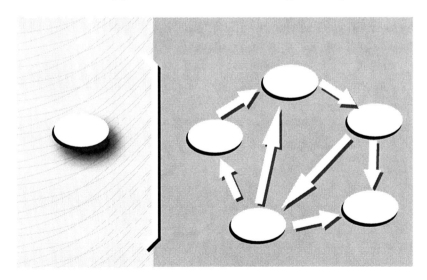

assumption

12. Absence of a System

YOUR BOARD, GRANTORS, INVESTORS, AND COMMUNITY ALL PUSH you to improve your fundraising. You ask yourself, "How do I get better?" Indeed, you'll receive brochures and flyers on new software, training, and other stuff along with ways to help the process and improve your pitch. Now, the pressure is on you to go out and make it happen. The key analysis here is for you to understand why the results do not match the intent. There are only three reasons you do not raise money, either you don't want to, you're mind says it's not possible, or there resonates a lack of system to follow. If you're willing and the results are not coming from your actions, then you need a proven system to follow. You want to avoid the common training approach called "passing it along" process or "the secret circle," and learn directly from the source.

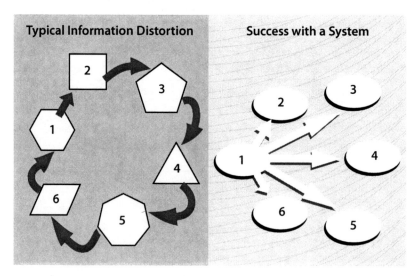

I've made assumptions in the prior section regarding the challenges you may face, but now we'll do some quick assessments to determine your starting point. As the short story below illustrates, you can get in trouble when you make assumptions. I saw this story on Sunday morning many years ago and do not remember the names and only have a brief synopsis.

The Assumption Story

An older man, about 85, would ride his bike up and down the streets of a medium sized town. His clothes were old and warn and his bike out of date and rusted. He would pick up cans by the bag full take them to the local recycle center and collect his change. Then he would donate the change to several local groups. The local people thought he was a poor, homeless person with one women quoted as saying, "wow I always thought he had a mental issues or something bad had happen in his life.

When he died he donated $5.8 million to the local church.

"Life is short - ASK A LOT OF GOOD QUESTIONS."

Let's figure out your FIRE by completing the BURN Assessment. Read through each sentence and then check off rarely, sometimes or always and at the end count how many times you checked always.

1.   I write out my personal goals each week and then connect them to the NPO goals

     Rarely_____   Sometimes_____   Always _____

2. I ask my prospective donor/sponsor about their charities and passions before I talk about mine

   Rarely_____ Sometimes_____ Always _____

3. I customize my 59 second commercial depending on who I am talking with

   Rarely_____ Sometimes_____ Always _____

4. I block out 15 to 20 hours per week to just do fundraising activities

   Rarely_____ Sometimes_____ Always _____

5. I use a fundraising system with specified steps to engage investors

   Rarely_____ Sometimes_____ Always _____

6. I provide business cards to everyone that touches are NPO

   Rarely_____ Sometime_____ Always _____

7. I use a tickler system to help me invite contacts to participate in cultivation models

   Rarely_____ Sometimes_____ Always _____

8. I use the two to three pain points that my NPO solves during discussions about the organization

   Rarely_____ Sometimes_____ Always _____

9. I offer my network more than donations to avoid the giving trap

   Rarely_____ Sometimes_____ Always _____

10. Our NPO completes a quick fundraising exercise during our board and committee meetings

   Rarely _____   Sometimes_____   Always _____

How Good Nonprofit Officers Become Great Fundraisers includes seven strategies with over 50 tactics incorporated, that when implemented will improve your FIRE as an NPO professional. The Fundraising Fire Formula and System brings out the FIRE in you to help improve the fundraising efforts of the entire NPO. If you have identified with the one or more of the assumed challenges that most if not all professionals' face, then you can start to make the transition from good to great. This transformation is not easy, but it is obtainable and is about IMPROVEMENT OVER PERFECTION©.

The strategies are built off of the five pillars of FIRE, incorporate real world activities, simple changes, and innovative thinking and include concepts, solutions, and tactics that will improve your individual contribution and in the end help the organization hit major goals and exceed expectations.

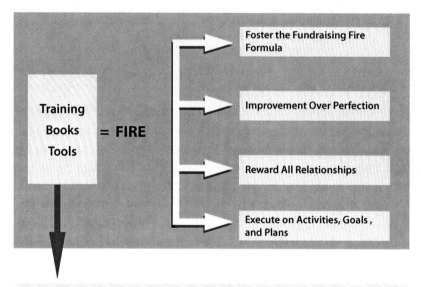

Fundraising Fire Course at the How Good Become Great Academy (Fundraising Fire Course) is an 8 week course and productive for both new Officers or helps veterans stay on target throughout the year.

FIRE is about expanding your passion, receiving help when you need it, and becoming great/a person of impact. You are the difference.

F   *F stands for Fundraising Formula.*

The number one priority of an NPO staff member whether you are the Executive Director, CEO, Development Manager/Officer/Director, Office Manager is to provide funding to the NPO so services can be provided to the end client.

The formula is:

$$CQ+P^3 = FUNDS$$

Represents the five steps each and every prospective donor or sponsor will go through as their deciding whether
or not to work with your organization. This formula is
simple to learn and remember, but not easy to implement. You will need to understand how each step relates
to the next one and sell yourself on utilization. The NPO
needs you to provide new processes, tools, and innovation
for it to survive and thrive. The value of the formula is
critical, often hard to define, and makes the difference
between success and failure. Through training, role playing, and authenticity, you will begin to experience different results, create positive case studies, and re-write
old mental (money) scripts. Fundraising models have
changed, but have you changed?

I stands for Improvement Over Perfection.

I Perfection is defined as high degree proficiency,
skill or excellence and the state of becoming perfect can cause severe trauma to both your mental capacities and physical body. You often find yourself
frustrated from the act of perfecting rather than improving. You end up avoiding certain behaviors because you're
not that good at them yet. Evaluate the details of what is
being asked of you and if you understand the NPOs expectations. If you do then you can start to improve your
own skills and knowledge, elevating your own individual
contributions. This is not about being a cheerleader, but
rather using enthusiasm and tools to motivate you and
your team members to raise the bar, expect something
better, and know that they have support and resources to
fall back on when the typical problems show up.

R stands for Rewarding All Relationships.

R Investors, Staff, Donors, Sponsors, Cheerleaders and Superstars love appreciation and while

some like cash and prizes others go for fame and portfolio bullet points. The key here is to show your gratitude to each and every person you come in contact with, understanding what scares, motivates, and moves them. Relationships grow similar to plants where water is exchanged for appreciation, fostering long term connections with the underlying rule of always giving to get (G^2 Formula). It is often as simple as saying thank you or sending a hand written note each and every time there is an opportunity. In other cases, you may need to send a gift certificate or tickets to an event. Either way, you must connect to every contact that helps or even attempts to help you or your organization. To further state this point, appreciate and thank everyone all the time, every minute, every second. This is a simple concept, but overlooked again and again.

E stands for Execute.

E We are often asked to take our contributions to the "next level" but next level means different things to different people. Execute means to carry out or accomplish a plan or order. This means to perform or do what you said you would, committing to walk the walk not just talk the talk. This is your chance to rise to a higher place or state, promoting the overall fundraising objectives not once a month or quarter, but in every interaction. The NPO you represent is looking for you to execute and offer more in the way of collaboration, knowledge, processes, and relationships, but they can't always articulate their needs or how to put you on the path to production/reaching those goals. You must listen, interpret, and then act. Great fundraisers are developed by great, properly trained people - it is just that simple.

Igniting a Blazing Fundraising Fire

"You can close more business (& Fundraising) in two months by becoming interested in other people than you can in two years by trying to get people interested in you."

— Dale Carnegie

ALTHOUGH THE FUNDRAISING GAME IS AFFECTED BY THE CURRENT changes in business process, economic decision making, technological innovation, social interaction, and political and cultural preferences, you can raise your contributions and reach levels of funding never before seen by the combined activities of improving your individual skills and implementing a fundraising day-to-day behavior system. You are the key to whether your organization survives and thrives or dies; not to put any added pressure on you of course. In fact, you are selling something more important than any traditional business product or service. If you do not utilize a system in which you can customize the tools and process to your personal style, preferences, and wiring, then you will continue to be stuck at your current fundraising levels. This is your chance to learn a process that helps you when obstacles show up, pushes you when motivation lags, and stops you when the best next move might be a step back rather than a step forward.

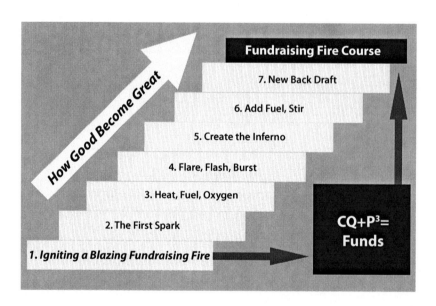

element

1. Fundraising: The 11 Letter Bad Word

"WE'RE RUNNING OUT OF MONEY," A DEVELOPMENT OFFICER SAID TO me during a meeting last year. Unfortunately this wasn't the first time I had heard this statement or one like it from a hard working, committed NPO (Nonprofit Organization) professional. Executive Directors (EDs), Development Officers/Directors (DOs), CEOs/VPs, Internal Staff members, Board Members, and volunteers all take on the challenge of the socially-responsible part of our society and they're typically involved with something great; something that moves people, a cause to stand behind, a moment to be digested, yet they are running out of money and resources. Why is this happening? I asked this leader what was causing this situation and her answer was, "we're still struggling with fundraising like every nonprofit." The answer was partially true, but also false.

There are of course many factors for lower than expected volumes of donations, sponsorships, and in-kind trade including economic issues, weak management, competitive forces, and lower than expected donations. Many are struggling just like Jacksonville, FL area nonprofits who laid off 35% of their staff last year[4]. However, as an NPO leader you have to focus on what you can control which is your style (attitude), expertise (skills), talent (activities) [SET Model] and let the rest go. My experience as a volunteer watching DDs/DOs and EDs as well as my own day-to-day fundraising activities helped me realize that the biggest challenge is not the economic or business factors, but the leader's definition of and their attitude towards fundraising.

The Development Officer continued, "I don't have time to get everything done and the pipeline of potential donors is shrinking." This NPO leader was struggling similar to other nonprofits officers around the country because of the lack of the right tools. This goes way beyond all the new and many cases great cultivation and flow systems and requires new strategies and tactics.

Most officers are attempting to fundraise by playing the "guessing game" with success based on trial and error. They try to learn how to fundraise from co-workers, free online newsletters, two hour sessions, or one day workshops. Even the EDs and CEO interrupt the information and then attempt to teach their staff, board, and volunteers. The challenge is that they pick up some good ideas here and there, but lack a system to follow on a daily basis. In fact, it's no wonder that Boardsource[5] reports that fundraising is the number one NPO issue by far, outpacing strategy, governance, marketing, and board development all together.

---

[4] Source: www.jacksonville.com
[5] Source: BoardSource Report 2007, National Center for Nonprofit Board

Let's face it; if you're a Development officer or ED, then you're frustrated. Your going out to the market place with less tools and prospecting more knowledge than your counterparts in the for profit world. Whether you realize it or not, your attitude towards fundraising affects everything you do. This is a sales game and you cannot sell your organization's vision, success rate, or value without a positive attitude. The obstacles you're running into are common place in the NPO sector and a negative attitude bleeds over into all the key segments of your donors, sponsorships, events, and creative tools.

Your current struggles tend to push into personal money scripts and beliefs. It comes down to long-time organizational culture issues, and connects to personal vision and goals. In fact, many officers try not to talk about their ineffective fundraising efforts, act as if hiding it in a closet somewhere will make it go away. They treat it like a terrible step child or awful first job and often wait passively for news on grant applications or direct mail campaigns with strong negative emotions conjured up when the results do not match the intent. Both Internal staff and Board members address fundraising, but more like a necessary evil than an opportunity. Now is the time to start active fundraising strategies versus passive strategies.

The first spark in igniting a blazing fundraising fire is shifting the mind set of not only the Executive Director (ED) and Development Director (DD), but their internal staff, board members, vendors, clients, and anyone who comes within 10 feet of the organization. When you change the attitude and cultural of your entity from a "have to" fundraise theme to a "want to" fundraise culture, you take a giant step towards new growth, opportunities, and success. You can make this leap to a new commitment which brings excitement, impact, and enthusiasm to your vision. In fact, you can shift the entire culture with some simple steps.

A great example of this type of shift comes from the corporate world. Nordstrom's took a part of business seen as a necessary evil and turned it into an incredible opportunity. Nordstrom's is one of the most successful retail companies in the world. Why? The answer is a complete shift in the attitude and delivery of Customer service. Not just good customer service but probably the best in the world without regard to industry or location. They changed the mind set of each and every person employed or connected to the firm. Their model is about going above and beyond at all times in every interaction.

In their book, The Nordstrom way, authors Robert Spector and Patrick McCarthey site that Nordstrom's culture encourages entrepreneurial, motivated men and women to make the extra effort to give customer service that is unequaled in America. In fact, they site Morley Safer on 60 minutes saying, "Not service like it use to be, but service like it never was." They continued the profile suggesting that "it is a place where service is an act of faith." The authors site Harry Mullikin, former Chairman Emeritus of Westin Hotels and Resorts quoted as saying, "If all business/entities could be like Nordstrom it would change the whole economy of this country."

Many NPO leaders could learn from Nordstrom and listen to Mr. Mullikin's quote because if all NPOs would change their attitude towards fundraising, then it would turn the entire NPO industry upside down. Nordstrom's changed what was previously viewed as a necessary evil, customer service, and placed it number one on their business strategy priorities. In fact, it has gone from a "have to do it," to their number one competitive advantage.

Implement a system to begin changing your attitude and belief towards raising money and you'll realize the power of fundraising – all the incredible things it can do for your organization and change it 180 degrees no matter what you have accomplished up to now or the state of the economy or the resources at your disposal. It doesn't matter what the situation, the change starts with you. You have to make the paradigm shift identified in **Element 2 and change the culture of your entity** or as Wayne Dyer says, "If you change the way you look at the things, the things you look at change."

element

2: The Paradigm Shift

"WE'VE BEEN USE TO THE OLD WAY OF THINKING, WE NEED TO expand our vision," I shouted out almost accidently at a board meeting. The other directors looked at me as if I had lost my mind, but the reality of my thinking was that if you don't shift your paradigm now it could be too late to grow your organization later.

The term "paradigm shift" became popular vernacular in the early 1960's due to Thomas Kuhn's book "The Structure of Scientific Revolutions"[6] where he used the term to refer to a theoretical framework. Marketers have grabbed on to the term especially in the technology and financial industries to describe a major shift from "the old way of

---

[6] http://www.des.emory.edu/mfp/Kuhn.html

thinking" to the new. Our own personal paradigms help us function in modern society; understanding how tools work, how situations should be handled, proper structure for relationships, and expectations of both career and professional development. Major changes in society like the current state of the world cause us to shift our paradigms. For example, the most recent recession has caused fear never before seen and elevated panic levels beyond recent recollection.

In fact, Wall Street Journal[7] article/quote referenced in the introduction and others like it, give justification for NPO leaders to simply give up, shut the doors, and find a new career or try a shift. It is true that the NPO world has been hit the hardest in comparison to many other industries with less government and private grants, some donors giving less and corporate giving down 75% in some cases. This has helped fuel a negative perception of NPO's questioning their ability to help or hinder society. This has lead to a major assault on not-for-profits where the prosecutors have become private citizens and corporate leaders who no longer see the relevance in some NPO programs. The amount of competition and overwhelming needs continues to add to this attitude shift. In fact, some states have one NPO per 200 citizens with many of these organizations seen as poor entities in crowded and competitive categories with unimportant missions extending their hand out as far as possible for funding and potentially wasting tax payer and corporate kindness. Furthermore, the new governing bodies have questioned and started to examine whether NPOs should be protected from tax issues. This pressure is bipartisan, coming from both sides of the political spectrum.

---

[7] Robert A. Guth, Wall Street Online 2010

The shift has been gradual but is picking up speed and the reality of the new fundraising world has only shown a movie trailer. We have not seen the true impact of the new economy or change in attitude to date so the long term effects are yet to be defined. Also, all the organizations that will close shop down the road have yet to be determined or revealed. The reality of fierce competition and more government restrictions may cause many more nonprofit entities to shutter.

Now is the time for you take action and understand the paradigm shift you must incorporate individually first and organizationally second in order to succeed and counter any movement happening in the world. In fact, you must treat your NPO like a for-profit organization (of course following all the rules and laws of your nonprofit legal category ex: 501C3) making improvements to every part of your business, but especially the tools and means for fundraising.

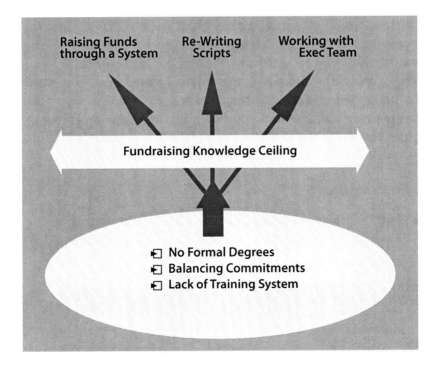

The shift comes when you change the attitudes and language, defining your entity as a real business that needs to produce an objective return on investment (ROI).

In the new NPO world, you must start calling your donors, sponsors, and supporters investors. Similar to a for-profit entity, anyone who touches your organization is an investor of some kind. Words like stakeholder are good, but investor points out the true magnitude of the relationship and reflects the seriousness of your new approach.

You no longer can rely on the "feels good in the heart" approach or show videos that make everyone tear up. These are great tools that are overused and should work in tandem with objective results. The new paradigm is related to a culture change that starts with you, extends to your staff, envelops your board, and climbs up to your donors and clients. This shift is about showing ROI through objectives means, establishing FUNDRAISING goals for everyone in the organization and demonstrating to the world why you're different. You must differentiate your group and demonstrate competitive advantages. You want to make the greatest difference for your customers (the people or animals that you help) but without more funds your vision will die. Here are some statements that could start the shift.

A Few Shifting Thoughts

- 90% of the time money is not the issue for your investor
- The more you act like a typical nonprofit the more resistance you can end up facing
- Strength Sponsors Strength

- Knowledge, Experience and Passion can reduce your funding
- Prospective donors/sponsors hide their true thoughts to protect themselves and their entity

There are several other shifting thoughts which I will cover throughout the book. The time is now to challenge your current perception of fundraising and create new scripts and a positive culture using **Element 3, Play Your Position**.

element

3: Play Your Position

"WHY WOULD WE DO THAT?" WAS THE INITIAL RESPONSE FROM MY board when I suggested that our foundation Board of Directors and members all have business cards. They were not overwhelmingly in favor, causing most of the members to give an odd facial expression and say, "Doesn't that cost money?" In fact, many for-profit companies and nonprofits are surprisingly stingy with tools like business cards even though it is one of the most fundamental, simple, and cheap ways to get everyone engaged in the fundraising game.

The reality is that every person in your organization, especially your board, is a key player in this new fundraising game whether they realize it or not. In fact, they are a representative for you whether they're at work or play; making contact with people all day that can help your efforts. They become a free fundraising (sales) rep. If you properly train the team and empower them with key tools like the business cards, then you'll see fundraising numbers increase dramatically.

There are many other tools and ideas to help the process, but shifting the entire organization's attitude and connection to fundraising is paramount. In fact, one of the misconceptions in the NPO world is that only the Development Director (Manger, Officer, etc.) is responsible for raising money. I had one DO whisper to me that a board member and an internal staff admin had both commented on multiple occasions, "why am I helping with fundraising, isn't that your job?" Although their main function is to raise funds, the DO or ED in many cases cannot be left on an island by themselves to fight a lonely battle. Their motivation can either be improved from watching a culture development in which everyone participates or decreased greatly when they realize that it's all on their shoulders.

The trend of having everyone involved in business development or sales has pushed many for-profit corporations to create incentive plans to leverage and motivate all employees to help with sales, referring potential customers and receiving cash or prizes for the assistance. In fact, according to a University of Melbourne Study[8], a high percentage of for-profit firms are looking to social media tools to help their employees sell and market their products and services. The questions here is do all of your staff and volunteers have some kind of connection to your organization via Face Book, LinkedIn or Twitter? Couldn't your strate-

---

[8] http://uninews.unimelb.edu.au/news/5750/

gies benefit from the staff's social interactions; markedly a blurb about your organization on their page(s)? You could be missing several great opportunities. This doesn't mean that they are selling on each and every point of contact, but if they are trained correctly they know when the opportunity is right. This seems like such a simple concept yet most NPOs do not properly train, arm, or empower their staff and volunteers to make it happen.

One of the challenges that you face is that you're unable to offer cash, bonuses, stock, etc. in order to entice your internal staff or volunteers to assist. You have to create a culture where everyone is pushing the fundraising culture forward. The question is how do you do this?

You do this through training and utilizing tools like the business cards. This helps everyone understand that the fundraising position is in everyone's title and job responsibility. It starts with the overall goal, moves into techniques, and then enters the incentives. You make sure each and every person (even volunteers) learns how to spot an investment (donation or sponsorship) opportunity which fits the overall objectives of the new strategy. Next, you offer simple (fun) training to get everyone up to speed; teaching techniques to see and take advantage of opportunities. These are short and simple webinars and in-person coffee get-togethers (if possible). Lastly, you creatively come up with incentives for the team, within laws and legal guidelines and motivate them to have a conscious awareness of beneficial situations.

You can even take it to the next level and have people write things on business cards or other material like, "We'll send you a free book," (you decide within the rules and legality) or something of value "if you call or e-mail our NPO I receive a free coffee for being a great team mate." Now when asked by potential donors/sponsors or people outside your NPO how many people are in fund-raising, you'll say **everyone**.

As you and your organization make the shift from a Good fundraising organization to a Great one, you'll need to fos-ter **Element 4, Give to Get,** to make sure your results reflect your efforts.

element

4. Give To Get (G² Formula)

ONE OF THE MAJOR COMPLAINTS I'VE HEARD FROM MANY INVESTORS is that, "the NPO only contacts me when they want something." Typically they phrase it like this, "they only want me for my check." Some investors will say this out loud, but most keeps it inside, having the affects of the feeling influence their impression and involvement with your entity. It's the thought in their mind of how you (the NPO) could help them (the investor) rather than how they can help you. This influences the referrals you receive and the in-kind trade (Power partners) opportunities. Of course they want to make a difference which is why they give, however, the subconscious thinking is, "What's in it for me." Now is your chance to give before you get and implement tools like the Golden Rule and Emotional Bank Account; thinking like a talent scout to help potential fundraising sources.

A well known saying is "put yourself in their shoes." How often do you really think about your investor? Do you really try to walk a mile in their shoes? In today's social media, with billions of bits of information, conflicting messages, and a trillion ways to market, your investors are getting approached by many sources. The number of "asks" they receive in person, via e-mail or by phone has gone up considerably in the last five years, but the methods for approaching them has stayed the same. Frankly, the pitch and methods are old and tiresome and it's time to try a new formula and realize that it comes down to quality approaches versus quantity.

Zig Zigler's famous quote, "You will get all you want in life if you help enough other people get what they want," is about focusing on what's in it for the other person. We could customize this quote in the NPO world to, "Your organization will get the donations/sponsors that you target if you help enough investors get what they want." Zig's quote connects into giving to your investor before they ever give anything to you.

As you look at your fundraising goals for the year, you need to change your mind set. It's not about what you or your NPO are going to get, it's about your willingness to give. We've all heard the saying, "you have to give to get," but most of us don't take it inside our heart and analyze what it really means to know how we can really make significant changes to what we focus on. You'll need to take an interest in your key supports, get to know them (I mean really get to know them not just superficially), and give to them in many different ways. The problem isn't that you don't know this strategy already. The challenge lies in how you've forgotten it or how you lack the tools to deliver on it. As your organization grows and develops, your own driving forces, goals and priorities become top of mind. You forget the importance of the formula. If you want to improve your fundraising efforts, simply think "give first".

This goes beyond providing heart tugging stories and reduces the time you spend on asking and inviting. This formula will keep you out of the giving trap and avoid the perils of requiring instant gratification. And by giving to get you will build strong relationships that will have significant value to you in the long term. The goal is to give more value to as many people as possible before they even consider giving you and/or your organization anything. This is often accomplished through tools like the Golden rule and the Emotional Bank Account.

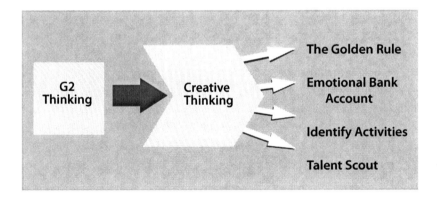

According to Wikipedia[9] "the Golden Rule is an ethical code that states one has a right to just treatment, and a responsibility to ensure justice for others." You'll also here the phrase "The ethic of reciprocity," used when describing the rule. It is arguably the most essential basis for the modern concept of human rights, though it has its critics. A key element of the golden rule is that a person attempting to live by this rule treats all people, not just members of his or her in-group, with consideration. You can apply

[9] www.wikipedia.com web site

the rule in your role as an NPO Officer; using your knowledge and imagination go ahead and take a few moments to understand the effect your actions have on the lives of others. Now imagine yourself in the potential investor's place on the receiving end of the action. It sounds so simple but is often overlooked so remember the Golden Rule during all your interactions.

A second key tool in the G^2 Formula is the Emotional Bank Account. This is a metaphor used to describe the give and take of most relationships and for our purposes, provides a way to build more trust in any professional relationship. There several ways to make deposits and withdraws in this set up including seeing people through their eyes and observance of the little things. As the saying goes, "little things equal big results". In fact, people typically make improper withdraws from others when they do not keep their commitment or they have different expectations. If you want others to help your NPO then make sure you are making regular deposits into the emotional bank account of your relationship, including saying thank you, sending over articles or ideas, keeping track of their kids or families lives and following through on any commitments you make.

Specific G2 Formula Activities

- Learn something special about each person in your network
- Find out what your potential donors care about
- Seek to understand what is important to your current and prospective donors
- Offer to do something for the investor right at the time you learn about their priorities

- Give them ideas, resources, leads, referrals, introductions, in-kind trade
- Find one way to help them by researching their firm, personal background or hobbies
- Create new fields in your database called "What's in it for them" (WIFT) or "Personal Preferences".

In the end, positive behaviors towards your prospective donors and cheerleaders results in deposits in the Emotional Bank Account and negative behaviors become withdrawals.

Another tactic is to begin seeing yourself as a talent scout similar to the judges on American Idol. It is still one of the most popular shows on TV with some 30 million people tuning in each week to see the good, the bad and the embarrassing. People also tune in to get a glimpse of the great undiscovered talents. The creators of American Idol and the four judges (or talent scouts as some might refer them) of the show have an amazing formula that can be transferred to the NPO world and by following this formula, you will be giving to your NPO before you get anything in return.

A talent scout must keep their eye on up and comers in the field, visiting sites to identify new people of interest who may not be on the scout's radar. They are often looking for specific talent. Likewise, you need to keep an open mind as you interact with others on a daily basis identifying who might benefit your NPO. As a leader, you're on the lookout for the next undiscovered talent who can bring incredible value to the organization and potentially add to your efforts; replacing the amazing value that exiting board members and volunteers contributed, and helping your investors with their key projects and goals.

There are both young and mature members of our society waiting to be discovered (recruited) to make a difference. In fact, some have direct connections to the organization as either clients or family/friends of clients or have indirect ties that make them a great candidate. When you create a culture of giving first and asking second, you differentiate your organization from all the rest. In fact, you'll notice investors coming to you rather than the other way around and this improves the chances of a successful implementation of the **Fundraising Fire System described in Element 5.**

element

5: The Formula that Ignites

"WE HAVE A TRAINER FROM BACK EAST COME IN ONCE A YEAR to meet with our staff and board," an NPO officer said to me recently and I said, "and its working?" She just looked puzzled and said, "NO." There are almost as many fund-raising systems, processes, and software as there are people attempting to use them. They are all great, but the key is for you to find the system that works best for you on an individual basis. The analogy I use comes from the weight loss world and comes down to "there is not cookie-cutter diet because we're all wired differently with specific health issues and unique metabolisms." Similarly, as an NPO officer you must find a system that works for **you**.

Indeed there are cultivation models, flow chart systems, donor pulls, donor drops and sponsor attractions. You name it and there is some type of process out there for engaging with potential funders. They are all great, but the key differentiation of the Fundraising Fire System is the focus on **your** individual day-to-day fundraising style, expertise, and talent.

Most systems run into problems when you consider the importance of identifying the right prospects and moving them from potentially interested investors to Super Star (Strategy 6) investors. You have to understand how to properly ask, invite, engage, and close investors. In fact, my system incorporates for-profit sales techniques with tested and true nonprofit approaches. I've spent many years raising money in both worlds and learned what worked and what failed. I use for-profit terms like prospect, close, present, etc. You have to start thinking more like a for-profit fundraiser because if the prospective investor does not give you money (buy your product), then your organization will no longer exist. You have to start thinking like a business development person, tracking your activities, understanding the current step and evaluating the next correct move.

The Fundraising Formula $CQ+P^3$ = Funds is the foundation of the entire system and this book and incorporates all the techniques and activities you need in five simple steps. This system is different than many of the outdated, passive methods, which lack the teeth to make it over obstacles. Furthermore, most traditional training has been taught by incredibly smart PHDs and consultants who have not had real life for-profit and/or nonprofit sales experience or training. You often end up caught in the drama and confusion of the Secret Circle or Pass It Along game.

The secret circle is the situation where key information is transferred from one person to the next. One person attempts to train or teach a system to the next person, similar to telling a secret, and that person passes the secret on to the next person and on and on (1 to 2 to 3, etc. in diagrams below). In the diagram titled Typical Information Distortion, the secret is nothing like the original by the time it gets around to the person who started the circle. This is similar to the fundraising skills and goals of most NPOs. The recipient takes in the information taught to them by a fellow staff member or ED/CEO, attempts to translate it (see change in shape with each person) and then passes it along to the next person. Each person in the circle gives it their best effort to listen, interpret, and then teach. The problem is that with each transfer, information is lost and distorted. At this point, you have one hand tied behind your back before you even go out to raise the first dollar. Besides, the NPO Officer is bogged down with training other staff members when they should be working on other tasks.

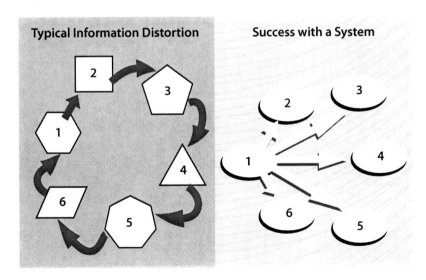

This circle with distorted shapes shows how information gets changed and a new version is created with each person. The end result is that internal staff members have the passion and drive to fundraise, but lack a sound, tested, and consistent system taught by one source as reflected in the Success with a System diagram. The NPO ends up underutilizing abilities of key staff and missing key goals. In fact, many internal staff members become confused, frustrated, and de-motivated. They often let their poor results or eventual resignation letter speak for the situation.

The Success with a System diagram (above) demonstrates how everyone can learn the same process and information from the same source, eliminating the distortion that happens with each step in the secret circle. The training is consistent, credible, and cutting edge, enabling staff leadership to focus on fundraising activities and improving their own talent level rather than wasting time trying to teach and train others.

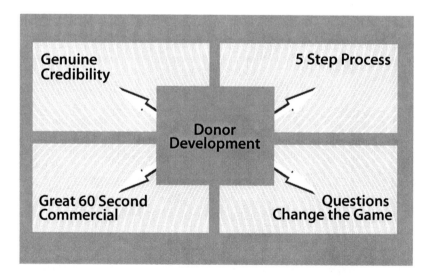

Similar to every other industry, the world of fundraising has changed and there are better ways to receive donations, sponsorships, and in-kind (Power Partner) contributions. Just like improvements in technology, materials, and teaching, fundraising systems have evolved. Today it is more important than ever to follow steps that lead to long term success. Besides, you are offering something less tangible than a house, car, technology, etc.

Your role is to fundraise and due to all of your other commitments, you only have a set amount of time each day or week for this activity. You must provide value and if you're stumbling through without a process, attempting to learn from ill prepared fellow staff members or board executives, then you're wasting what little time you have to help.

You don't need, nor do you have the time, to learn a complex way to bring in funds. Therefore, your team must use simple tools to clearly define the organization's fundraising expectations to create a fantastic 59 second commercial, to offer consistent reinforcement, and to improve each person's level of contribution. It's time for a system that incorporates all the modern positive attributes of the for-profit training process with the innovation and customization required for the nonprofit world challenges.

This book and Fundraising Fire Formula are built on core pillars of FIRE discussed in the introduction and the five steps involved in the Fundraising Fire System (FFS). This system is based off of my real life experience. Of course obtaining sponsors and donors is not the same as selling traditional business products or services; however, there are several tools and innovative approaches that cross over in both worlds and I've incorporated the advantages and dropped off the negatives.

This system is simple to learn. The formula CQ+P3 = Funds stands for (C) Confidence with proper (Q) Questions plus (P³) Power, Presentation, and Partnership can equal tremendous levels of donors and sponsorships (i.e. lots of funds). The five steps eliminate the need to guess your next action or implement ineffective techniques.

The main point of the CQ+P³= Fund process is to provide you with a guide or a way to walk your potential investor through the five steps. You'll not only know where you are during the process, but you'll feel confident of where the relationships should go to next. It's time to fill up your pipeline and avoid wasting time with people who will never donate, sponsor, invest, or provide value. Indeed, you need to focus on matched investors, who agree with your mission and understand your value proposition.

$CQ+P^3 = FUNDS$

Confidence	Questioning	Power	Presentation	Partnership
Build Trust	Focus on Them	Empower & Clarify	Match solutions	Create relationships
→	→	→	→	→

C *Your Confidence in yourself* increases their confidence in you. Establishing a close emotional bond with another person is an incredibly important step and can be done in seconds with the proper training and tools. You can also lose trust in seconds if you are unable to overcome hurdles in the process. We all know that people do business (donate and sponsor) with people they like, trust and view as being "like them". In Tim Sanders book, *The*

Like Ability Factor, he points out that George Gallop has conducted a personality factor poll prior to every Presidential election since 1960 and "only one of three factors –issues, part affiliation, and likability – has been a consistent prognosticator of the final election result: likeability."

You increase your chances of signing on key investors if you increase your likability by having Genuine Credibility habits and mirror or match them. Your ability to manage and create new mental scripts, identifying your burning life vision, knowing your own strengths, and analyzing and articulating your own goals help the prospect feel something special, comfortable, confident, and calm.

Your confidence or lack thereof becomes a critical part of obtaining investors and in-kind (Power Partners) trade. People can sense when you feel comfortable and passionate about your organization or if you're fake and shallow. Your confidence allows you to listen and match the speed your prospect talks, the words they use, their physical movements, and the way they dress. This process deals with the world of NLP or non linguistic patterns.

NLP is an acronym for the three most influential components tied in producing human experiences/emotions – neurology, language, and programming. According to the web definition, the neurological system regulates how our bodies function. Language determines the kinds of models of the world we create. NLP programming describes the interaction between the mind and language and how that interaction affects the body and behavior. NLP helps you understand someone when their words are either not clear or perhaps misleading. For example, you might tell the sales associate that you're interested in purchasing something in a retail store, but your body is facing the door with facial expression making you look like you need to go to the restroom (miss signals). Or there are times when you connect with another person right from the second you meet or talk to them. The more you understand how NLP works, including your own behavioral preferences, the faster your comfort level grows.

The more comfortable you feel then the more sincere interest you can have in the person your interacting with and the more value you bring to their life. For example, if, while talking on the phone, you can follow their dialogue speed and speak either louder or softer depending on their style, then you can connect, bond, influence. In fact, the more comfortable you make them feel; the more confident they'll be in your NPO and their ROI for investing in your group. Improving confidence starts with knowing yourself.

Your personal strengths play into how you interact with others and when you identify them in Strategy 3, you begin to see why your good at what you do or why you may be falling down. Emotions in others influence the type of engagement or communication that takes place. The more you understand how your wiring interacts with the wiring of others, the more it helps you create a stronger bond.

The C part of the system covers all opportunities and challenges within each person to properly interact with prospects. This includes their mental scripts, expectations, beliefs, goals and vision. The first step in selling, closing, obtaining, receiving buy-in, or fundraising is building confidence in yourself and in your prospect.

Strategies & Tactics I teach:
Genuine Credibility (Strategy 4)

StrengthsFinder (Strategy 2)

ASCEND Process (Strategy 2)

The Green Light Process (Strategy 2)

NLP Styles & Behavior (Strategy 3)

Once you have worked on your own wiring you will begin to notice and evaluate the wiring of others. At this point, you can move on to the next part of the Formula – Questioning.

Questions change the game.

Q You'll find that most people talk too much. In fact, it's not quantity but quality especially when you consider that the Gettysburg Address was 272 words while the average USA Today article is 1500 words and your NPO conversation is probably 2000 words too many. If you're talking then you're not fundraising and your coming across more like a Doctor prescribing remedies when they haven't heard the symptoms.

You might have been taught or trained to have a great pitch, articulating the features and benefits of your organization. A well constructed, dynamic pitch is important but understanding when to bring it out and when not to use it is critical. In fact, a great 59 second commercial opens doors and a poor one or lack of one keeps them closed.

The questioning process starts with a great commercial and extends into open ended questions that keep the focus on the prospective sponsor or donor. Your intro/commercial doesn't pitch anything but rather it starts the WIFT tactic. You no longer have to ask for anything specifically, but your style and type of questions produces the right answers without confusion or drama. If you want to be different, then act different. In fact, if you want to fundraise then ask questions – don't tell or direct anyone to do anything.

Example questions include (There are 12 powerful questions you can ask – four are below):

- What types of organizations do you give your time or money to?
- What do you look for in NPOs?
- How much money do you typically give each year? (Budget & Investment Questions)
- Who do you know that might want to help our group?

You want to think like a doctor, detective or reporter. You're interviewing the prospective donor/sponsor - You're not selling anything. You'll notice that most of the questions listed above are based on facts as well as opinions and impressions. You goal is for them to start formulating a flow chart of information, desires, things to avoid, etc. You're attempting to get to their real feelings with a trust level that avoids the Iceberg Phenomenon (Strategy 3).

Everyone wants to feel important and that their opinion matters, so help them feel good. Take them into the future and ask about what would be ideal or what could be improved; covering what has not worked in the past but what could work in the future if properly changed.

Great questions help you avoid making the wrong assumptions and identify critical data like who the decision maker is or how many people will influence the yes or no answer. Furthermore, the right answers to the right questions make matching prospects to your ideal investor profile easier; often saving you unnecessary presentation time.

The third step, P^3, helps you identify the prospects decision-making process, what benefits you should present, and how to grow long term relationships (creating Super-Stars and Power Partners)

P3 Power, Presentation, Partnership

Yield the Power - you need to find out how they make decisions and who else influences their choices. However, you have to lead this part of the process, keeping them in the driver seat with you as a gentle guide. The key part of this step is asking good questions indirectly but not creating an uncomfortable atmosphere by asking direct questions. For example here is a key question: When you've invested (donated or sponsored) in the past, how did you know you'd made a good decision? The use of the word investor in this question can help you differentiate. Or who do you trust the most to help provide additional ideas? This process empowers the prospect, helping you uncover hidden information or unseen decision makers waiting in the wings to douse your fire.

In addition, POWER also means developing Genuine Credibility (Strategy 3), attracting the right investor, and leveraging your board members' and volunteers' POWER (Strategy 4).

Play the match game -If you were listening (and taking notes is highly recommended) during the Q (or Questioning) part of the formula, providing authentic behaviors and empowering those around you, then matching the solutions to the problems becomes easier. The prospective donor or sponsor may not care that you've been around for 100 years or that you have had the same staff for 10 years. They told you their concerns when you asked the proper questions so now match your solutions to those answers. Take the canned presentation you've had and customize it to each prospect you deal with and connect their needs to your value. Lastly, keep in mind that most investors need to know immediately how you're NPO has a better ROI than another one or what makes you the Pink Cat (Strategy 3).

This is your chance at this point in the process to "pitch" as such, but if you were a good Doctor or detective then should know what benefits will entice your prospect. They'll think to themselves, "Wow you really hit all of our concerns and opportunities." This result occurred not because you're a mind reader, but you asked great questions and then listened for the answer. You matched their desires, objectives, and needs to your NPO's value.

__Creating long term relationships__ -Partnership is defined as "a relationship between individuals or groups that is characterized by mutual cooperation and responsibility, as for the achievement of a specified goal." You're looking for something more intense than just a front-line relationship. In fact, you want a partnership where you provide help and assistance and receive it back. I call these Power Partners because they offer not only money but in-kind trade, referrals, creative resources, and new opportunities. In fact, investors often become partners in the process as well, often providing Power Partner-type solutions along with their investments.

In a great relationship you can ask honest and at times difficult questions. You need to do some post close work at this point. This means you've discovered what success looks like from them or you've articulated their expectations. If you feel there will be a potential problem with their donation expectations or sponsorship follow through, then talk about it right now and get the details out on the table before the issues arise.

In the end, make sure you get to the key issues and even prevent some problems by identifying potential landmines before you or the prospect step on one. Tools such as a proper tickler system, SuperStar form, and the NPO Leader Fundraising Time System will help you foster great partnerships. As you move on Strategy 2, The First Spark, keep in mind that your number one focus is improvement over perfection. The Fundraising Fire System starts with you so go ahead and light the Spark.

Strategy 1 Summary

- ↵ The paradigm shift start with you
- ↵ Change Fundraising from a "have to" to a "want to"
- ↵ You have to give first to get second
- ↵ Everyone connected to your NPO is playing the fundraiser position
- ↵ The CQ+P^3 = Funds Formula is the key system for you to incorporate and utilize to improve your individual contribution

Key Action Steps
(You Can Do This Right Now):

1. Write down the current fundraising systems/tools you currently use and next to each one answer yes or no as to how effective they have been

_____

_____

2. Print up business cards for everyone in your entity (board members, volunteers, staff, etc.)

_____

Tool:
*CQ+P^3=Funds Formula Card

*Available at HowGoodBecomeGreat.com

strategy

2. The First Spark

"To believe in the things you can see and touch is no belief at all. But to believe in the unseen is both a triumph and a blessing."

— Bob Proctor

YOU MUST UNDERSTAND HOW YOUR PERSONAL LIFE VISION AND goals affect your contribution to the fundraising efforts of the organization you represent and how they either align or don't align with the NPOs mission and vision. This is about working on your own abilities because your role in the NPO world is even more important today than it was yesterday. You want to connect what is most important to you and what you do on a daily basis to the mission of the organization. The key is writing out your goals, identifying key style (behavior) numbers, and pursuing your NPO dreams with reckless abandonment. You are selling a key value to the improvement of our society with your actions; causing major ripple effects for all of society. The reality is that in order to get better fundraising results, you have to get better and for your organization to change, you have to change.

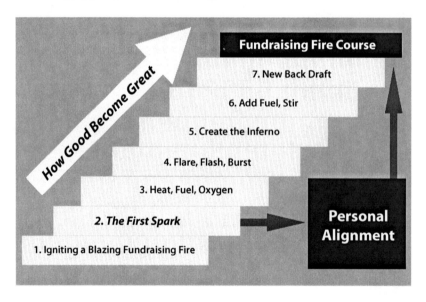

element

6: The Green Light Process

"I WORK IN MARKETING NOW, BUT I'VE ALWAYS WANTED TO MAKE movies," Steve said to me the first time I met him at a networking event. It was an interested opening statement, unique but perplexing. He said the statement almost with a futuristic knowing, as if he had been working on his own mental scripts. Later, I would help Steve as the Executive Producer to make that movie (Seclusion – Available at Netflix or Blockbuster) and learned some valuable lessons about mental scripts from the movie industry that I took over to my volunteer and fundraising roles.

In the movie business when they green light a project it means their moving forward into the production phase; kicking off a whirl wind of activities including signing the director, bringing on executive producers, and hiring the cinematographer just to name a few of the chores. At the green light, those behind the movie believe it will be successful and their actions match their belief.

As a NPO leader, the green light process deals with how you create new scripts, beliefs, and expectations with regard to your own fundraising activities and behavior. In many cases the Borrower Phenomenon© (Discussed in the Assumptions Section) appears over and over when people have not written new mental scripts regarding asking for money or inviting a contact to attend an event. You often stop when approaching a potential sponsor because the feeling of rejection starts to come over you or you're influenced by the existing scripts of the current staff, board, or investors.

The Borrower Phenomenon is similar to watching a homeless person ask for money and it affects many areas of your organization including day-to-day operations, goal setting, and sponsorship structures. The same type of mental script as observing a homeless person solicit money from strangers begins to play in the board member's mind. They begin to feel unfortunate, lost, confused, or overbearing. They wonder within if the person they've approached will frown upon them for asking for their attendance or asking to sponsor an event. These feelings have nothing to do with the person's real psyche or with the importance of actually asking people for assistance, but naturally come on when they are put in the uncomfortable position of asking for anything relating to money. Even if you are an exception, you still deal with strong money scripts when you tackle your prospecting responsibilities.

Money scripts fall into three main areas including the amount of money considered to be a lot of money, where the money comes from, and the way in which it is obtained.

These scripts are mostly subconscious, but can be addressed with new ones written at the conscious level. Money scripts come from many sources including family, friends, jobs, community organizations, school, and media. Your parents probably created some of the strongest scripts when they said, "little one, you never ask other people for money – it's rude." Or they said the most critical word of all, "NO". They had positive intentions however they caused you a life time of issues when it comes to fundraising.

More specifically, with your prospecting time the scripts can be even stronger because so much of the value you offer is intangible and emotionally driven and it can be looked at as bothering (or begging) others just by inviting them to help (close the deal). Most people have no idea how many scripts are influencing their life until they stop and think about it. These scripts often dictate your fundraising results without you even knowing it. One example of how these scripts impact you are to take the effect of watching a movie especially one in a theatre setting.

Have you ever cried at a movie? Or become intensely scared? Excited? You knew the movie was not real yet the script, the characters and the flow made you feel something. Stand up in the theatre and go touch the screen, look behind it and you'll see that it is a wall with no bogeyman or hero standing there. Your mind can not differ between what was vividly imagined and what was real for the two hours you sat in front of the screen.

Similar to a movie, your scripts cause you to react in certain ways, often times in ways that do not benefit your actions nor help you reach your professional goals. Your fundraising efforts could be hampered by the negative scripts that keep playing over and over in your mind. For example, if you've never brought in more than 4 **SuperStar**© donors

(Strategy 6) per year, then you may have a script playing in your mind that reflects four as your maximum.

One of the key solutions to your mental script challenges is to set a high reaching yearly personal fundraising goal and do the same for your staff. You must be assertive when establishing these goals whether it is for you internal team or board; offering to have open dialogue with them about money scripts. Indeed, expanding the goals and discussing the meaning of each one helps, but you need to make changes through tools like the Money Game, Positive Self Talk, and Gratitude Forms. These help change negative scripts into positive ones and fill in a positive experience when you're most recent fundraising efforts might have left you disappointed and frustrated.

The Money Game - is a great way to gage your initial script about money. From your viewpoint, how much money is a lot to fundraise? Write a number in the box on the next page– write in whatever comes to you first or what you feel in your gut. Now ask yourself, "Why did I put the amount in the box that I did? It is correct?"

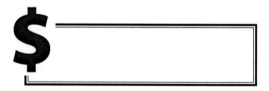

"It is my true feelings or did someone or something influences the amount I put in the box or could prior results be affecting my future outlook?" Just by identifying this number you start to realize your first problem.

Now take the number you put in the above box and multiply it by 10.

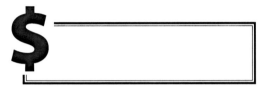

How do you feel about the new number? Not realistic? If so, why not? Start to think about what it means for the organization to hit this new number, evaluating all the gains, benefits, opportunities, and new clients served by reaching this number.

According to Tony Poderis, who's been in the fundraising game for 30 years, "Unfortunately, far too many non-profit organizations refuse to acknowledge that the development department performs what one could argue is the most important function in the organization. They give short shrift to its needs and the staff to accomplish them. They hire entry-level people and expect them to perform the work of accomplished professionals, or they ask accomplished professionals to work for entry-level wages." If you're like many Development and Executive Directors/Officers, you've become trapped by what you have accomplished up to today.

Your mental scripts influence all of your activities, relationships, and resources and are based on the top number or the highest level of your current money script. If the number you wrote in the bottom square of the money game didn't seem real, then you're caught at your Donation Threshold Level©. This threshold occurs when you build your ideology around your current resource model and circle of influence. You'll need to shift your thinking and evaluate the x10 number you put in the second box in order to break through and utilize new tools to meet new investors (people/contacts) that can bring the higher donor and sponsor value to your group and develop networks where contacts provide larger donations.

Even though corporate and foundation giving, government grants and fees for service are down, there are still a plethora of opportunities to grow new revenue channels, identify new ideal investors, and sign on more small to midsize sponsors. The problem is that they haven't given to your organization because they have not been asked or not asked in a proper fashion. That is one of the key script challenges in the NPO world; NPO executives and staff afraid to do enough prospecting activities to accomplish larger goals.

When you shift your paradigm by writing new scripts, your first step is to change your attitude. You must approach the process with positive energy, enthusiasm, and a willingness to change. In fact, you make your NPO responsibility top of mind, drinking the Kool-Aid as such because your 100% committed to seeing the entity succeed. You've identified your money expectations by completing the money game and you're ready to move forward, remembering that it is about IMPROVEMENT OVER PERFECTION.

Louise Hay, founder of Hay House Publishing and author of the book *You Can Heal Your Life*, which has sold more than 35 million copies throughout the world explains, "Your beliefs and ideas about yourself and the roles you play are often the cause of our emotional problems and physical maladies." Saturday night live actor and writer Al Franken took a shot at self talk via his character Stuart Smalley, "I'm good enough, I'm smart enough, and doggone it, people like me." The irony of the spoof was the truth in it. If your heart does not believe the words you express then you probably not taking the right prospecting action and wasting your time. In fact, your potential investors will know if your invitation or ask is genuine and authentic. They'll feel it in their heart when you come from a position of knowing how to properly ask and invite and doing it in a method that reflects confidence.

You change your behavior by shifting your paradigm and aligning your personal vision with the mission and stakeholders of the organization. This starts in your own mind and although this step is sometimes looked upon as fuzzy or "new age," it provides a gateway to understanding not only how you do something, but why you do it. You start to connect to the mission of the NPO you represent by defining **Element 7, Creating a Burning Vision**.

element

7: Creating a Burning Vision

"THIS FOUNDATION CAN GIVE AWAY \$1 MILLION DOLLARS PER year." My famous statement to my board back in late 2005 was an opportunity to help our group make a giant mental leap. Besides, we were all volunteers and we had nothing to lose and hundreds of thousands of kids to help. After they responded with several comments suggesting that I was crazy and that it was impossible, I continued on to explain my burning vision. I explained that over three years, carrying the theme of "$1 Million for The Kids," we could reach the goal. Of course we would have to change some tactics and techniques, but the new vision if lit properly would end up causing a fire storm of new attitudes. We ended up tripling our fundraising numbers to just shy of $1 Million in those three years and in the process I discovered another way to create the fire inside.

For one to have a life vision they must look deep within their own soul to see what really matters to them. Your own personal vision can get your fundraising on fire or suffocate any potential flames. What is important to you? The organization you represent has a vision, but does your personal vision match it.

We all have to-do lists, projects, and roles, but do our goals match our dreams. Are you working on the activities that will bring the best ROI (Return on Investment)? You also have challenges and situations that either push you to improve or cause you to fall back. You have to continue the passion that helped you start, become a team member of, or take the leadership role of the NPO you represent today. If your life vision doesn't match the organization you represent or has significantly changed then you're setting yourself up for disappointment and shifting paradigms or attitudes becomes almost impossible. Why are you raising money? Is it just for them? Or is it something deeper, something that stirs you, wakes you early, keeps you up at night, and leads to incredible personal growth.

The foundation of successful fundraising comes down to aligning your personal passion and goals with those of the organization. In fact, most people are unaware of any misalignment between the organizations goals, values and beliefs until a later point in the relationship and if you were once aligned, but now disconnected it's time to revisit your personal vision.

Alignment is the connection you make between the key objectives of the NPO and your own and includes understanding your rights, obligations, other staff member's values, and expected activities. Most research shows that organizations fail because there is not an alignment between the previous mentioned issues and the internal team, board members, clients, and/or volunteers. For example, if you've had a negative experience with fundraising, then you struggle to have a burning vision when you confronted with new fundraising challenges. The past problems that lead to your frustration could exist with the new initiative so correcting those issues should not be underestimated.

On the other hand, you avoid the borrower phenomenon and achieve alignment when you know your own strengths and wiring along with your personal goals and beliefs. This connects your behavior to key results and raises your motivation. Lastly, your commitment level is solidified when your personal vision is aligned with mission of the NPO.

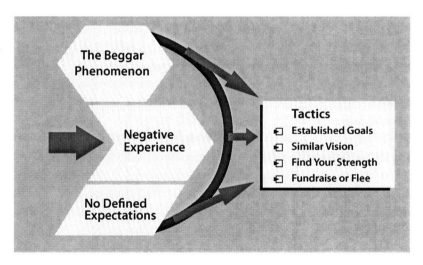

Creating a vision and becoming a great fundraiser comes down to completing some simple self analysis steps including evaluating your own ability to listen, analyze opportunities, think clearly and creatively, work well with others and lead by example. You're willing to prepare for key meetings, ask the right questions of prospective investors (often difficult questions) and sponsors, contribute resources, open the right doors, and develop and improve fundraising skills that you may not currently posses.

A "burning vision" is created when you properly assess your personal strengths and fundraising abilities, establish written goals, and evaluate current beliefs. Then you can choose the appropriate actions for helping. The next step is to identify your strength in **Element 8, Find Your Strength.**

element

8: Find Your Strength

THE FAMOUS GREEK DELPHI SITE HAD THE WORDS, "KNOW THY-self," inscribed on the Temple of Apollo. A friend of mine pointed out that the Latin version of this thought is written on a plaque above the Oracle's door in the Matrix film series. The point was in order to evaluate and help others, you have to understand your own strengths and figure out the methods to making them stronger. You say fundraising is a weakness, but do you understand the reasons why you're struggling? After completing a self assessment, you may find that it is (or should be) a strength of yours. You need to identify why you're doing some prospecting activities while avoiding others.

If you're going to improve your fundraising skills, you need to find out what you're good at and which areas cause you to struggle. This is where self analysis plays a key part in the process. If you understand your own wiring, you'll begin to better understand the people around you and increase the donations and assistance they provide.

The first step is to take the BURN Assessment©. The NFL has the combine and the Olympics have the trials to determine the athletes starting point, ranking to others, and likelihood of organizational fit. We use the BURN assessment to help you evaluate your fundraising talents, fire inside, and personal alignment issues. I created this assessment to help identify an NPO leader's starting point in the fundraising game.

BURN is an acronym meaning:
Current **B**eliefs
& **U**nderstanding **R**esponses
Nurtures behavior

This process was created from real world experience and involves answering a few questions to have a better understanding of your current beliefs, responses, and behaviors. The results show both you and the NPO where you are starting from, what strengths you can improve on and potential obstacles you'll need to overcome. This assessment is not about true or false answers, but provides a snapshot of the person's opportunities and potential value and helps the NPO understand the person's starting view point. You can bring a ton of value if the NPO knows how to utilize your talents properly and help you make adjustments to their process.

Another important step is to purchase the Strengths-finder 2.0 book (http://strengths.gallup.com/) and take the strength assessment. Both the Wall Street Journal and USA Today listed this book as a best seller. It takes about 20 minutes to complete the assessment and you'll appreciate the results; helping you start the process of identifying why you may not be raising money for your NPO. The authors spent several years researching how people can identify their own talents and as the Strengthsfinder system describes, "Do you have the opportunity to do what you do best *every day*?" "Chances are, you don't. All too often, our natural talents go untapped. From the cradle to the cubicle, we devote more time to fixing our shortcomings than to developing our strengths." You can add in that using the tool to uncover your talents and to find out why you're struggling with certain tasks.

> All How Good Become Great
> Academy Attendees take the
> Strengthsfinder Assessment

Another great tool is the DISC tool offered through several sales and management consulting firms. The DISC® is a personality assessment that helps you gain insight and better understanding into the strengths and challenges of your behavior style. You must take a moment to find out your strengths so that you can start to improve your activities. After you understand your own strength you can focus on the ASCEND process which is a step by step system to accomplish your life vision and major goals. This process is in place to help you with **Element 9 or "ASCEND-ing" Your Personal Mountain**.

element

9: ASCENDing Your Mountains

"IT'S TIME TO CREATE YOUR GOAL BOARD," COLLEEN SAID WITH A grin. She is a great sales coach and mentor with professional characteristics, deep values, and a drive to succeed. The class began working on our boards, cutting pictures out of magazines and gluing them on to a large white poster board. We spent two or three hours talking about goals, dreams, and living an exciting life. It was a great experience.

The first time I brought this concept to a NPO, they looked at me with very strange expressions. They were thinking the same thing I was thinking, we could identify with the pictures and place them appropriately, but there was a lack of a process for accomplishing the life visions. In fact, there was a gap between the end goal (picture) and the steps to get to it. We weren't even sure how to set the priorities for such a goal. Once I decided what was most important to me, I would need to connect them to the groups and businesses I was involved in and the important people in my life that would be affected by the goals. Therefore, I created my own process.

As our yearly vision board sessions have grown from just Karen and me to many people, I realized the importance to having a process to define the end results. Each year the process I have developed called ASCEND – the acronym stands for Attitude, Spirit, Connection, Evaluate, Navigate, and Development – has evolved. This is about accomplishing your most important dreams and reaching the vision of your life similar to climbing a mountain. I cover this tool in the first class at my Fundraising Fire Course to identify your own goals. Along the way, after establishing your own goals, you start to understand where your goals align with your NFP organization and at what points you're disconnected.

Each step in the process transcends one mountain (or obstacle) to the next. As you reach the top of one, the next becomes larger and more challenging. In fact, you have to take it one step at a time, overcoming problems and finding unique pathways. As an NPO Officer, the vision of raising a $1 million per year can seem impossible if you only currently raise $250,000. However, if you make it through all six stages, then you'll have a great start to understanding your starting point and along the way, you'll discover a way to get to the fundraising levels that you once thought were impossible. You'll feel empowered knowing your connecting your behavior to your goals. It takes about 2 to 4 hours to complete the entire process, but it will save you years of frustration.

IMPROVEMENT OVER PERFECTION starts with your own goals, dreams, and beliefs before you can help the organization take a giant leap. The diagram below shows the process.

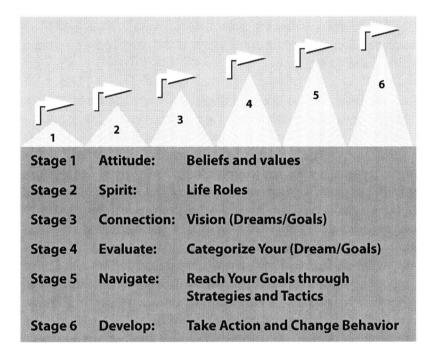

Stage 1	Attitude:	Beliefs and values
Stage 2	Spirit:	Life Roles
Stage 3	Connection:	Vision (Dreams/Goals)
Stage 4	Evaluate:	Categorize Your (Dream/Goals)
Stage 5	Navigate:	Reach Your Goals through Strategies and Tactics
Stage 6	Develop:	Take Action and Change Behavior

As you stare at the top of the highest mountain of your vision, you probably feel different emotions running from two extremes; excitement to fear. Questions pop into your mind like, "How in the world am I going to achieve that? Is this really my life vision and do these goals belong to someone else?" Naturally you'll go back and forth, often spending seconds at each extreme then collecting your thoughts and composing yourself. NPO Officers often avoid certain prospecting activities because those activities are not in line with their personal goals or vision. In this case, the most important step is the first one – write out your ideal day.

The ideal day exercise is a tool I picked up along the way that helps you grasp your time and values. Here, you are identifying who you want to spend the most time with and what you would like to do with that time. This is a motivating exercise because you're connecting your daily activities to your ultimate goal or end result. The key then becomes how your fundraising activities help you reach your ideal day?

Accomplishing new goals is about how you spend each day. Are you avoiding your most important fundraising activities? Are you focused on the big picture and key tasks that enable your organization to raise more money? It's about listing your day on an hourly basis to identify where you might be wasting time or spending time on projects and tasks that do nothing to push you or your organization's values and goals forward. What is your ideal day? This exercise is about identifying your ideal day, in the present, with no limitations or requirements. Life is not about just existing, but about the pursuit of your dreams. Here we are trying to avoid Emerson's famous quote that "most people live in quiet desperation." What if your day were 100% your choice? Actually it is your choice; but perhaps you let all the other influences, problems, and people impede or take over your day.

In this exercise, money doesn't matter nor do your roles or responsibilities – it's about what you want to do; not what you think you have to do. Grab a pencil or pen and fill it out - Fill out your ideal day. No limits. It's up to you. It's your Vision for your life! Do it right now! Don't wait.

IDEAL DAY EXERCISE	
6:00 AM	
7:00	
8:00	
9:00	**E-mail info@billyounginspires.com and ask for the Ideal Day Form**

Summary of 6 Steps Follows: (Details & Implementation provided at Fundraising Academy)

 STAGE 1 OF THE ASCEND PROCESS

Attitude = Beliefs and Values

Do you believe you can raise the money and hit the goals you need to hit? Do you believe you can meet the people you need to meet? What about bringing in the sponsorship dollars to keep your event or group moving forward? Start with clarifying your beliefs of who you are and who you are not.

I like to challenge people with the following questions:

- Why are you doing what you're doing?
- Are you following your own passion or someone else's?
- Are you passionate about the NFP?
- Why do you believe what you believe?
- What forces influence your beliefs? Parents? Bosses? Donors/Investors? Government? Friends?

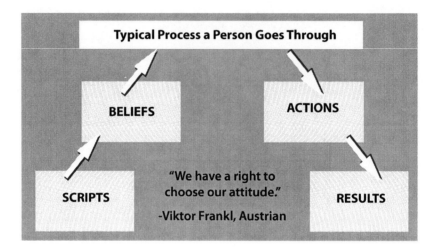

Your belief system controls the way you interact with investors (donors), co-workers, etc. Does the talk about the economy create excuses for you? Do you accept less from investors because of the economy? Do you show up late and leave early because you believe you cannot change your circumstances? What is controlling your attitude? Typically our habits along with certain fears and mental baggage play a key role in how we react to each day and each event in our life. Are these beliefs real or outdated? You might have beliefs that are flat out wrong or not true.

 STAGE 2

SPIRIT: Join Your Life Roles to the NPO you represent

After identifying your beliefs (and clearing out what others believe), you can clarify your life responsibilities. We all wear many hats in the game of life. While some of us have just a few roles – friend, son, and granddaughter - others have many. All the different roles you play affect how you interact with donors and your time is limited so what you spend it on effects all the areas of your life. Are you spending your time on accomplishing goals that fit into your highest priorities? Many people spend time in their low priority roles while ignoring the most important areas. Does your current role in the NFP cause you to spend time with people that will never donate to your group? By clarifying your responsibilities, you can match your life vision to specific roles (both personal and professional) and spend time with the people that mean the most to you.

A few examples of the roles you play may include husband, wife, daughter, boss, dad, leader, coach, community helper, Development Officer, etc. Now, take a moment and identify all of your life roles. You want to identify those roles, key people you are responsible to and how you can improve your interaction with them.

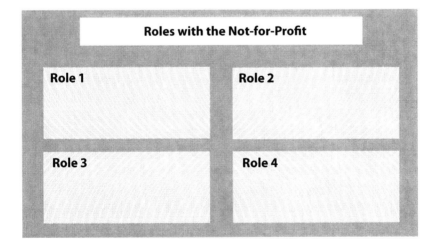

You've climbed over mountain 1 or Step 1; attitude, and made it up the cliff of number 2; Spirit, where you defined your roles, therefore, at this point your ready to face Step 3; Connection.

STAGE 3

CONNECTION: Connecting your mind to the vision

As children we're taught that our imagination is important with no limitations or boundaries. As adults we're conditioned to be "realistic" and to take our "heads out of the clouds". We're taught to not waste time on our dreams, but rather just take what we are given and exist. Go to a job, pay your bills, and don't cause any waves. A great passion or life desire can help you overcome this process of demotivation. In fact, one of the best movies ever made was Shawshank Redemption (original book written by Steven King). The main character, Andy (played by Tim Robbins) in an important scene describes to Red (played by Morgan Freeman) his vision of his life when he gets out of prison. Red responds by saying, "You need to stop doing this to yourself." "That life is out there and you're in here." Andy responds, "Then I need to get busy living or get busy dying". The amazing part of this exchange is Andy's unwavering commitment to his vision. No need to ruin the ending of the movie for you if you haven't seen it, but Andy's mind is focused on his vision and dreams while his body is trapped in a 10 by 5 foot cell.

The power of writing down your beliefs, goals, and life vision is beyond explanation. Study after study reveals that when you commit to writing down your goals, you move yourself into the top 5% of people in our society yet the numbers still show that most people do not establish or write down their goals.

Mark McCormack's book, *What They Don't Teach You In The Harvard Business School*, tells of the famous Harvard study conducted between 1979 and 1989. The finding of the study (and often used statistic) was that 3%

of graduates who had clear, written goals when they left Harvard were earning, on average, *ten times* as much as the other 97% of graduates *all together*. The 3% number has probably increased to 10 or 15% over the last 20 years, but is still lower than expected.

The point is that if you do not understand your own goals then you probably won't be able to fulfill the fundraising goals of the NPO. You must write down your goals and then ensure that every person that touches your organization, albeit staff, board members, etc. establishes a fundraising goal for themselves at the start of the year. Each person's goals should be customized to their individual skills, talents, and opportunities. If they haven't yet established goals this year, then you must suggest that they take this step immediately.

The previously mentioned statistic is even more amazing when you think about the incredible results you can achieve when you put your thoughts on to paper. The words you write down stay on your mind and in front of you at all times. If you do not write them down, chances are you will easily forget about them. Have you ever experienced the "out of sight - out of mind" phenomenon? If you do not have a constant reminder of things you wish to do, be or have, you tend to easily forget about them. Jim Rohn, author/speaker, was dead on when he said, "If you don't design your own life plan, chances are you'll fall into someone else's. And guess what they might have planned for you? Not much."

As you look back at the path you climbed in Step 3, you'll feel confident because you've finished writing down your goals and connecting them to your defined roles. In step four you categorize them.

 STAGE 4 OF THE ASCEND PROCESS

EVALUATE: evaluate and categorize your major goals

At this point you've spent time reflecting on your beliefs and you've written down your goals, now you've decided to take action to accomplish your potential.

When you categorize your goals you create a concise pathway to achievement. The following is one example of taking one goal, drilling down and creating a stronger connection between the goal and reality.

STEP 4 Evaluate: Categorize Your Goals	
Example	
Major Goal #1:	*Raise $5,000 for NPO this year*
Key people that are part of it:	*Bob, Jane, Chamber of Commerce*
What could stop me from achieving it?	*Not asking them in a timely manor*
If I achieved it how would people it impact my role?	*I could help 100 more or 1000 more kids if I hit this funding goal*

Simply take each major goal and define three important issues including the key people that are part of your plan, what could stop you from achieving your goal and the level of impact on your life if you achieve the goal. In this step you are digging down into the goal to see what could help or hinder your progress, defining it earlier than later and helping reach step 5; Navigate. You're starting to make the goal real by defining necessary tasks.

STAGE 5

NAVIGATE: navigate with strategies and tactics

We've all heard this before, but what type of tools can one use to not only write them down but actually work them and in the end navigate the obstacles and challenges and reach the goals? W. Clement Stone said, "Whatever the mind can concave, one can achieve." One technique is to utilize a vision board filled in with your unique dreams and goals, putting into place the first step in accomplishing them (Discussed in the Attitude section).

Next you must identify your goals from a strategic view and understand what tactics will help you in your journey. At this point you've checked off the following tactics:

A Strategic view point – tactics include:

- Create vision board
- Define the goals for each dream
- Write them down
- Establish dates
- List the resources you will need
- Understand the steps and tasks
- Prioritize the steps
- Fit the tasks into your calendar
- Take action each day even if it's only for five minutes

Now that you have a vision sheet or board created, go a step further. Break each dream down into details and answer any key questions that emerge. You may not know how, but the clearer you become the more likely you are to accomplish your dreams.

Example:

⊡   Major Goal: Own a mountain home

    ▽ Key Strategy: Research locations and options

    ▽ Deadline: January 2009

    ▽ Resources needed: Internet access, personal preferences, data

    ▽ Strategies (Steps and tasks)

        ▣ Identify where

        ▣ Sketch out what the house will look like

        ▣ Research the area

        ▣ Establish a budget

 STAGE 6

DEVELOP: Develop an action plan and change behavior

According to Anthony Robbins, "You see, in life, lots of people know what to do, but few people actually do what they know. Knowing is not enough! You must take action." Now you've put your goals down and clarified your roles and values, and detailed out the steps to accomplish your biggest goals. What once may have been impossible is now real. Keep in mind that everything you see in the world was started with an idea.

There are two key daily tactics that help change behavior; self talk and gratitude tools. These tools help connect your beliefs and action plans to the actual behavior you complete or ignore each day.

Self talk is more about an attitude and what you say inside your mind than what you spout out to the world. It is not pretending like things are wonderful and saying words that you truly do not feel or believe in your heart. When you commit to self talk, you use phrases and words that empower you and connect your words to your beliefs. This is the recognition of beliefs in your mind that you may need to change or reprogram. As you change the self talk, you begin to believe the words and phrases that appear in your mind and to the outside world.

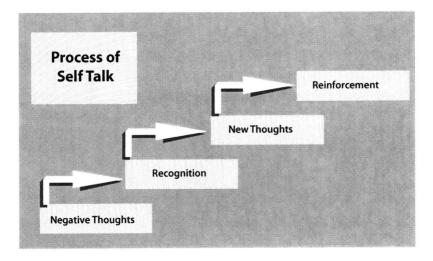

The first step is accepting that yourself talk is negative and is based on old beliefs. Next you recognize the thoughts when they occur – i.e. "The economy is too tough right now." After you start to recognize the negative tones and filter the ones that no longer work for you, you create new thoughts or write new scripts. Now you have replaced the "economy is too tough right now," thought with, "today I'll secure one new sponsor no matter what."

This is the point where you use daily affirmation or a gratitude journal. At the last level, you reinforce the new thoughts with consistent words, utilizing exercises on a daily basis. This includes placing the phrases where you can see them, i.e. "I am a powerful person who will gain a new investor today."

Self Talk Procedures and Examples

Self Talk Options and Examples
▣ Silent: Sitting quietly at a coffee shop or deep meditation
▣ Verbalize: Out loud to yourself or others or pay close attention to the words you use
▣ Written: Phrasing and writing in your words or letter format, journaling, bullet points
▣ Video: Record yourself saying it or film yourself discussing the goal

A Gratitude Journal (you can buy off of the Internet) or a NPO Gratitude Journal (Obtain at www.billyounginspires. com – free tools) provides a second tool for working on internal beliefs and behavior. You might have one statement that you write down each day or 3, 5, 10. The quantity of gratitude statements is up to you.

Today I am grateful for _____
(Fill-in this blank with what you are grateful for)

Examples include: my life, my children, my company, my work, my recovery.

Your creativity will expand as you use the tool more, evolving into statements like:

Today I am grateful for the time with my family and the presence that God plays in my life. I'm appreciative of my co-workers and clients and feel fortunate that I can help people on a daily basis.

Self talk is an important part of your life both personally and professionally. It can make or break you; influencing that what you believe is possible or not possible on a daily basis. You'll want to pay close attention to the words you think about as well as verbalize. Remember that affirmation or positive thoughts must be in the present, specific, and cause good results. The tools you use must be simple, easy to find (daily basis), practical and realistic. Lastly, you must evaluate if the self talk is really you and honest.

Here are a few more daily keys to taking action and changing your behavior:

- Established daily routine
- Planning your week on Sunday or Saturday evening
- Using a planning system (Ex: Outlook, Franklin)
- Writing in your gratitude journal
- Helping others
- Volunteering
- Weekly goal meeting
- Daily review of dreams
- Delegating work

The ASCEND process helps NPO leaders clearly define their goals and life vision in detail using a process and setting the stage for pursuing **Element 10, Reckless abandonment.**

element

10: Reckless Abandonment

"IF YOU TRULY BELIEVE IN WHAT YOU'RE DOING, THEN YOU'LL HAVE reckless abandonment toward your goals," Richard Brooke used this phrase during his vision workshop. His statement hit me between the eyes like a stiff punch. It was one of the factors that helped me create the Fundraising System and write this book. I was going along and not following my passion which is to train NPO executives, help board members, and speak to all types of groups.

Although the phrase "Reckless Abandonment," usually conjures up negative images and is tied to having no concern for the consequences of your actions or defined as the trait of lacking restraint or control, for our purposes I'm using the phrase to help you understand how you need to act in order for your fundraising levels to increase substantially. I'm using the term as a positive thrust for you to have courage to do the behaviors and activities that you must even though you may have fear or doubt about the final outcome. It's about working more hours then you planned or persisting until the prospective investor have signed on.

When you are enjoying your activities and tackling every interaction with enthusiasm, helping others with leads, problems, and opportunities, then you're acting with reckless abandonment. Hours pass without you noticing and you're following your goals and dreams and helping your organization accomplish something incredible, major, important, and necessary. The difference between you fundraising at $5,000 level or $5,000,000 has nothing to do with available resources, but it's your beliefs and activities that affect the range of funding.

Once you have an attitude of reckless abandonment towards reaching your goals and your actions match that intensity, you'll start to pay attention to new tools and incorporate better ways to bring on investors and combine the heat, fuel, and oxygen necessary to implement Strategy 3.

Strategy 2 Summary

- Our mental scripts are controlled by our thoughts
- Decide if your values are imposed or real (from the heart)
- Self talk influences your behavior which determines your attitude
- Write out your goals and then detail the steps and tactics to accomplishing them
- Goals are affected more by how you think then what you do

☑ Create a powerful personal vision that aligns with the mission of the NPO

☑ The better you know your own strength the more your fundraising will improve

Key Action Steps
(You Can Do This Right Now):

1. What actions are you going to take today in regards to your beliefs and Vision?

   _____

2. What is your fundraising Goal for this year (write it down right now)

   $ _____

Not checks you'll write – the dollars you bring in from all sources

Tool:
*ASCEND Kit and Goal Card

*Available at HowGoodBecomeGreat.com

strategy

3: Heat, Fuel, Oxygen

"It has always been my belief that a man (person) should do his best, regardless of how much he receives for his services, or the number of people he may be serving or the class of people served.

Napoleon Hill

YOU BEGIN TO IMPROVE THE WAY YOU IDENTIFY POTENTIAL DONORS and sponsors by defining your ideal (Perfect) Investor. There are thousands of people wanting to work with you however, they do not know who you are and you do not know how to find them yet. They need to know how you differentiate from other NPOs and the value you bring. You must change the culture of your NPO by adjusting attitudes, implementing new terminology, and creating a positive fundraising environment. In the end, trust between you and the investors comes through the questions you ask and a 59 second commercial that engages and provokes.

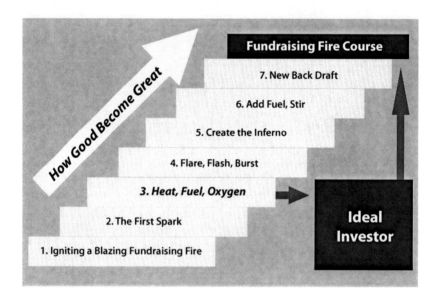

element

II: Identifying Your Ideal Investor

"EVERYONE SHOULD BE GIVING TO US." I OVERHEARD THIS COMment at a board meeting a few years back and although it was said with a strong positive reflection, it wasn't quite true. Your NPO is similar to for-profit organizations in the market place; they have an ideal customer and deal with the constant challenge of finding and engaging with them.

When you work with as many NPOs as I have you notice a few things from time to time including that most of them are focused on their own passion, clients, and community needs which is good, but can make them lose focus on what is often their most critical target when raising money — they are donors/sponsors/advocates/vendors (investors). People who donate or sponsor your events deserve the title of investors because they're making a contribution into something that they anticipate will have a return on investment (ROI); if not to them directly then to the community they live and work in. These investors are making a contribution to you in one way or another and they're expecting an ROI (either explicitly defined or assumed). The ROI may not come in the form of direct dollars back, although at times it does, but rather a return consisting of social impact, personal "feel good" rating, and local community improvement. Yes they want to see you financially strong, but most importantly they want a return as they see it or as they define it. Many of you are overlooking who your investors are, the importance of demonstrating your unique value to them, the WIFT (What's in it for them) formula, and the importance of connecting to their internal fire (passion).

According to Seth Godin, "Without a specific reason for the consumer (investors) to behave, without a reward or benefit, the overwhelmed consumer (investor) will refuse." I've exchanged the word consumer for investor in Seth's quote so that you get the picture – the investor is your NPO consumer. They may not get direct help from you as your clientele do, but they are the lifeline of your organization similar to how the customer of the local cable company keeps them in business. They need to understand, in a very clear way, why they should give to you and not someone else. If you can articulate who your ideal investor is and match your tools to their needs, then you can grow your investor bases, increase average donations, increase sponsorships, and expand your reach. Let's begin with the profile.

An accurate profile of your current investor is critical. First, start to consider the investor you want to attract in the future. Targeting or profiling the right investor is often overdone and oversold in the marketing world. If it is not done correctly or not done at all, then you'll spend a ton of time (and possibly money) pursuing old databases, mismatching characteristics, and chasing dead ends. Start changing your thinking from anyone that has a pulse to anyone that has the passion for our NPO. This includes the right corporate fit and the best contact within their organization for you to have the best results.

Many NPOs keep hitting up the same people with the same methods, getting no results or they don't try at all turning to passive actions. This activity sounds like the definition of insanity, doing the same thing over and over and expecting something different. A great profile starts with the process that you implement to identify who gives to you and how to attract more of them. As you begin the process, make sure you try to think of as many aspects of your investor as possible. Use the Fundraising Fire Profile process called FLAME to identify who your ideal investor is and what their most important characteristics include. As you identify the similarities, pull out as many charac- teristics and psychographics as possible. You'll soon have a profile of your ideal investor, starting the process of cre- ating methods to get more of them. At this point, you'll know who to target and how to find them.

The FLAME process stands for the following:

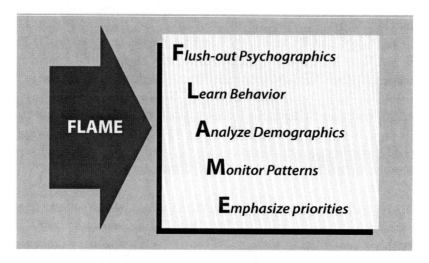

Flush out psychographics — There are plenty of marketing and strategy gurus devolving ideas about customer profiles, but for our purposes here we simply want a snap shot of who you're attempting to get in front of for donations, sponsorships, and in-kind trade (Power Partners). You'll start to identify, utilizing your current database, why donors invest in and/or sponsors sponsor your organization or to other organizations similar to yours. When you improve this part of your process you also improve the questions you ask investors and the data you will start to obtain.

In the field of branding jargon, marketing, surveys, and social research, there are attributes that fall outside the norm of the typically demographics. These IAOs as they are often referred, which stands for interests, activities, and opinions, are compared with demographics like age and location or behavior such as usage rate or devotion to a brand. Psychographics are separate from demographics, but work in tandem to drill down on who your customer/donor is and why they give to you. Furthermore, they tend to relate to personality, beliefs, attitudes, interests, or lifestyles.

For example, you'll mine your database to see if your current investors and/or contacts fit with any of the following: conformist, risk taker, conservative/liberal, fun loving, socially conscious, cutting edge, trend followers. You might be asking what if we don't know any those characteristics about our investor base. If this thought crossed your mind, then you identified your first project with improving and isolating your list. Besides, you're probably paying hefty fees for a NPO software/database system and they tend to offer you opportunities to upgrade or improve the system you use. Take them up on it during your next cycle by giving them additional fields to add –in some cases they'll do it for free if they can offer it to other NPOs. For now just take some guesses.

Typical categories include:

- Politics
- Environmental
- Social Issues
- Personality type

Here are some additional example psychographics:
Conservative, Liberal, Conformist, Experimental, Environment-friendly, Socially conscious, Fashion-forward, Growth-oriented, Fun-loving, Trend follower, Family-oriented Cutting-edge

In addition to personal influences take a look at the company they work for:

What are the key characteristics of that firm? Example - Number of employees, Year founded Location of head-quarters/size and number of branches, Types of products and services they provide, Annual revenue, private vs. family business

Learn Behavior— The next step is to identify what your investors like to do. This is the key part of your analysis. Figure out trends or similarities, i.e. Do 75% of your investors play golf? 50% ski? What hobbies and/or sports do your donors participate in? What publications do they subscribe to? What types of entertainment interests them? How do they spend their free time? If they're a corporate donor what growth stage are they in - start-up, growth, stable, or decline? Is there consistent industries? What type of employees do they have? (Young, old, contactors, family business) Who is the decision maker you're connecting with? What are the common characteristics of their executives? What is the management style like? What is the company's corporate culture? What trade associations do they belong to? If these questions cause you an upset stomach from an inability to answer, then you should attend our Academy (Class 2 covers Ideal Investor) or you just start with some simple information gathering questions and tools.

Analyze demographics — Continue to drill down and remember, the better you know your investor, the better you can serve existing ones the more likely you are to get more of them. We explain the power of creating cheerleaders and SuperStars later in the book, but for now take your top 20 or 50 investors and do the following analysis (Include both donors and event sponsors –if you do events):

- Age
- Gender
- Profession

- Education level
- Household income level
- Marital status
- Number of children
- Geographic location
- Other

Monitor Patterns — When you start to monitor their patterns of donation, you'll notice some additional trends such as when they donate. Do more donate in the summer versus winter? Are there seasonal issues? How about if changes occur after something happens? How long have they been donating? What benefit is the investor looking for? How often do they invest? What is the investor's decision-making process?

Here are the key factors that most investors identify with regard to picking the NFP to support:

- Donation level
- Quality/ROI of services
- Brand name recognition
- Customer service
- Variety of services
- Potential referrals and introductions
- Convenience of location
- Facility Appearance
- Ease of payment/Flexible payment terms
- Other

Which phrases from the above list are you consistently seeing from your investors?

Emphasize priorities — The last step to creating the FLAME is to emphasize the priorities – you're about to write out your ideal investor. You'll notice consistent patterns and fields. Once you understand the profile of your donor (the current one) you'll need to identify your ideal investor/donor. Look at the list you've compiled above and prioritize the all of the key categories, taking the information you've assembled and write out the description.

DATABASES AND TOOLS TO ACCESS PUBLIC SOURCES

Governmental Resources, Census Bureau, –census.gov or via telephone at 301-763-INFO (ext. 4636), Bureau of Labor Statistics Consumer Expenditures Survey –online at www. bls.gov/cex/home. htm or via telephone at (202) 691-6900, Libraries, Dun & Bradstreet and Standard & Poor's Company profiles, The Statistical Abstract of the United States, Encyclopedia of Associations, Encyclopedia of Business Information & Sources, Standard & Poor's Industry Surveys –Trade and Professional Organizations

All sources found via a Google search

The ideal investor for our NPO is (Top three descriptors)

🔲_____

🔲_____

🔲_____

Ideal Investor (Describe in detail)

_____

_____

_____

_____

Write in as many details from the FLAME exercise as you can. Once you identified your ideal investor you can move on to preparing a POWER partner sheet. This is a single piece of paper that you can provide to contacts that outlines your ideal investor/partner, describing their habits, concerns, and typical industries they work in and enable them to recognize opportunities for you. This entire process helps improve your interaction with prospects and sets up the ground work for using **Element 12, a 59 second commercial that sells.**

element

12: The 59 Second Commercial That Sells

"WOULD YOU LIKE TO ADD A PAIR OF SCISSORS TO YOUR ORDER, Jeanne?" I said while selling Cutco Cutlery in college. My results did not match my intent back in those days, but then my personal commercial was not very appealing either. In fact, during a long career of selling different types of business models and raising money in both the nonprofit and for profit environments which started with selling those knives, some success steps become very apparent like the importance of a properly crafted 59 second commercial.

Although it is often more difficult to carve out a great NPO commercial this step is still paramount to your success and overlooked by 98% of the NPOs in the country. This is not a TV or radio commercial, but you will want to begin to think like an advertiser because this commercial is the foundation of everything you do. It connects to your brand, demonstrates the clientele you help, and fosters ideal investors. This is the initial hook that pulls people into your objectives. It must be consistent, believable, and showcase the pain you stop or the benefit you offer. This is not only about discussing the types of clients you help, but the types of investors that fit your organization. The goal is to have the message speak for your group in a quick sound bite, creating curiosity. Even though the commercial can be challenging to initially establish, a sizzling one will help make lining up new investors an easier process for you, your board, and your internal staff. You'll need to fully understand the outline, the process of creating one, how it works, and when it is used in your fundraising process.

A 59 second commercial is the foundation to your benefit to potential investors. It starts the defining process of how the world perceives your organization. In fact, this significant first step improves your prospecting and fundraising efforts by 10 fold and begins when you assume that the prospect you're talking to does not know your organization or the value the organization represents. Even if they are familiar with your NPO, they may not know exactly the value you produce for the community. We often make an assumption that the people we're interacting with know our organization. Deliver your commercial acting as though they cannot directly help you, but their network, professional or personal activities, and who they know could offer assistance. This enables the commercial to do the work, taking the pressure off of a direct ask and focuses on their circle of influence.

It is called a 59 Second Commercial because it should be shorter than a minute if possible. In fact, the shorter, the better. Your goal is to cover within this brief time frame, what your organization does, who it helps and the benefits or challenges that can be avoided by donating, sponsoring or partnering with your NPO. It should not cover too many details, but offer a chance to hook people with the issues the organization solves or gains the organization provides. It is a movie trailer or quick preview. Typically the commercial contains two to three short sentences that flow off the tongue, get to the point and can be easily understood. You'll know when you have a good commercial because people will be proactive in their reaction and they will begin to ask certain questions.

When you start the process of creating your commercial you'll need to involve your entire staff and begin with your branding message, building from it but not dependent on it. There are three parts to the creation of your commercial. The first part consists of what your NPO does and who you help, including your name and org name making sure you don't use acronyms. Clearly define the name and the type of people or groups you help. Using "ETF" or some other three or four letter acronym may cause confusion if they do not know your entity by the abbreviated version.

Secondly, define the value you bring to investors. This step is easy for a for-profit venture because they offer some type of tangible product or service. You offer a service or product that has more value, but is more difficult to define. This is critical to the quality of your message; discussing how you help rather than who you help. As we covered in Strategy 2, answer the "What's in it for them" question. For example, if you provide assistance to children you might say, "We helped 10,000 kids stay alive last year and you may know one of them." This type of statement lends to your impact and the fact that the person you're talking to will appreciate that you helped those kids and they didn't have to provide the assistance directly. You're saving a lot of professionals a ton of time, money, and effort, so make sure they realize this when they meet you.

As your contact hears the commercial they should be thinking of how they can help you, offering introductions or referrals or providing help directly from them or their company. You may have to go through several versions before you come up with the right one. Make sure your staff and board (if applicable) are in agreement and that everyone commits to using the same commercial. This is your prospecting commercial not a TV, Web or other type of commercial.

A great 59 second commercial causes a pattern interruption for your contact and creates curiosity with clarity and opportunity. If they look at you with a strange expression as if their lost, then you need to work on your commercial. It should inspire them, not cause confusion. It tells what you do similar to the way a product commercial on TV explains their offer without all the details, teasing but not closing you. Furthermore, your commercial creates anticipation, much like a movie trailer does without all the special effects.

You should conclude with the action words at the end that help define how they can work with you or what types of resources or tools you are looking for them to provide. Try to experiment with this by asking for a specific referral. For example, you could say, "we helped 10,000 kids last year and now we're looking to meet someone in the C level at Microsoft." Ask for the help you need. You have 59 seconds (probably more like 30) to pull them in or become just another cause out there trying to do "good." Action phrases and words produce next steps while vanilla introductions leave you lost in the shuffle.

A great commercial starts the differentiation process for your entity and helps your audience understand not only your value in the community, but how they can help you. After you've established the commercial, you're ready to tackle **Element 13 by creating your "pink cat"**.

element

13: The Pink Cat

"WE NEED TO FIND THE PINK CAT." AFTER I SAID THESE WORDS, the board of directors (for-profit company) looked at me as if I had lost my mind. You would get people's attention if you showed up at their business or house holding a pink cat. Of course, there are no naturally pink colored cats but the phrase probably grabbed your attention and showed you the power of differentiation.

Differentiation in marketing is defined as the process of distinguishing a product or offering from others, to make it more attractive to a particular target market. In addition, for our purposes, differentiation in fundraising (NPO Investor Development) means how you individually utilize the uniqueness of your NPO with the characteristics that make you different as a person. This involves the way you act, look, and interact and the way your organization is perceived.

One of the challenges that most NPOs run into is either looking like all the other nonprofits or not clearly articulating what is different about their entity. In Seth Godin's book, *Purple Cow*, he talks about how the rules governing marketing are changing ever more rapidly as the world is changing. The old commercials do not work the way they once did and consumers have checked out or become numb. Seth writes, "You're either a Purple Cow or you're not. You're either remarkable or invisible. Make your choice." He continues, "Face it, the checklist of tired 'P's marketers have used for decades to get their product noticed -Pricing, Promotion, Publicity, to name a few-aren't working anymore. There's an exceptionally important 'P' that has to be added to the list. It's Purple Cow." We're using Seth's paradigm shift as an example but for our purposes, this book focuses on articulating how it is very different for a nonprofit versus a for-profit organization to differentiate itself, hence, the name "Pink Cat". Now is the time for your organization to become one.

So your first question is probably what is a pink cat? Let's start with a mental picture. Your walking up your drive way and you look over to your neighbor's house and you see a pink cat in their yard. As you proceed to walk over to get a better look, your reaction probably ranges from, "what in the world is that," to "I think I need some rest because cats are not pink." You may even go inside your house and lie down. Either way, the point is that you had a reaction. You experienced a pattern interruption. Even with all the mental images, visual advertising, and targeted messages (estimated at 1,600 per day for the average person in the US.[10]) sent your way each day, you would still notice the pink cat.

---

[10] 2007 Nielson Report

As an NPO leader you make yourself and your organization look like a pink cat when you identify unique characteristics of your group, create special appeals within your client base, and develop creative/custom approaches from yourself. First, articulate in one phrase what is different about your NPO in comparison to other NPOs and firms in the for-profit market place. If you serve a demographic that is highly competitive, then find that one (or more if they exist) characteristic(s) that make you different. Also, evaluate a firm in the for-profit space that is either very similar to yours or very different and understand and if possible copy the way they differentiate their firm. Next, identify in your client base a person, theme or thing that cries out with difference. For example, if you only serve tigers, then focus on what great thing about serving tigers will create curiosity and action from your target audience. Lastly, and probably most importantly, find your personal pink cat. This could be the way you dress, your style, the words you use, etc. When people interact with you they'll start to see and understand why you (not just your organization) are different and should be trusted, interacted with, and why they should invest in you. Some way to make yourself pink:

- Always wearing a NPO logo
- Dress in a suit
- Wear a special hat
- "Logo'd" shirt

Unfortunately one NPO after another try to emulate the traditional nonprofit "pulling the heart strings approach." In fact, it is almost impossible to attend a workshop or seminar where the training does not call for you to tell your most powerful heartfelt (tear jerker) story. This is great and can work, but everyone has seen it. They are numb to it and your organization looks like all the rest when this is your only approach because that emotional feeling wears off quickly when they get back to the regular world.

During your next fundraising meeting with your internal staff, discuss the characteristics that make your cat pink. As you create more differentiation in the marketplace you'll increase the trust others have in you, helping understand and utilize **Element 14, the Iceberg Phenomenon**.

element

14: The Iceberg Phenomenon

"TRUST IS IN WHAT YOU DO, NOT WHAT YOU SAY," I TOLD OUR SALES staff at one of our first XploreNet sales meetings. I was attempting to make a point on action versus thought and perception versus reality. Trust is a very subjective concept and felt with many different emotions from the trust you would feel with the paramedic as they take you out of a mangled car and your life is in their hands to the trust you have with your significant other or staff. There are actually similar trust levels that get ignited by different circumstances. The reality is that people protect themselves by only telling you part of the truth; not that they're lying, rather they are just not telling the entire story.

What are you asking potential investors to do for your not-for-profit? Many of you might find that you're not asking them anything, but telling them how great your entity is or how badly you need the money. Trust is about asking questions. Not just for the sake of asking, but using questions in the right method to identify the key issues for your investors. You are the doctor or psychologist in this situation, uncovering the reasons "to" or "not to" investment in your entity. You're a detective using tools to get to the truth.

I call the relationship system the FUEL system (Strategy 6). This system is a way of strengthening the trust you have with your current investor base and the type you target for new investors. In fact, you may not be developing the type of trust that you think you have with your prospective donors and sponsors and are experiencing the effects of the Iceberg Phenomenon.

I've found over the years that investors don't always let you know their real thoughts or agenda. We're all taught from a very young age on to hide some of our real emotions and convictions. Ever hear the saying, "don't ever talk about religion or politics with people?" Shouldn't that saying go more like, "make sure the person you're talking to wants to talk about religion and politics?" I'm sure I'm not the only one, but I like talking about those subjects and do not get easily offended.

In many cases your investors and prospects have the iceberg phenomenon happening which means what you're getting on the surface is less and in reduced detail as to what is underneath.

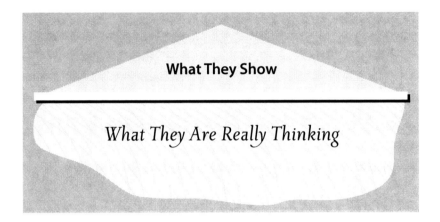

Are you asking the right questions in order to gage who your prospects are and what they think about? Let's help you figure out how to truly walk a mile in their shoes.

You want to ask a lot of questions –not redundant, boring questions but pertinent questions that help you understand the investor's mind set, including their fears, ideas, opinions, and beliefs. The questions you ask help walk them through your process. By asking questions, you take the pressure off of directly asking for help. A great tool for your questioning process is to use the SWOT analysis or in fundraising the FUND analysis (Fortitude, Uncertainties, Next steps, Dangers). Companies typically do SWOT (which stands for Strengths, Weaknesses, Opportunities, and Threats) on a yearly basis to gage their market position and develop long term goals. In our academy, we cover the FUND analysis in detail formulated to help you ask the right questions so that you have a better feel for whom you're targeting and how to understand what is important to them.

What are their strengths (fortitude)? Or what do they really care about? They typically have skills in areas that tend to lean towards certain biases and beliefs. They give to certain charities because of this skill level. For example, you might ask the question – what do you consider your (or your firm's) biggest strength? This question alone could have a 15 minute response. But take it further now by using this question in face-to-face meetings and in surveys that you send out.

Uncertainties (Weaknesses) are the next step and you might ask, "How do I ask you about your weaknesses (especially as a donor or supporter of the not-for-profit world)?" This is a loaded question, but your best method is to suggest that many of the donors that give to your not-for-profit end up staying with you for a long time. For the few that leave you become disingenuous, or just lose touch, there is a reason. Now tell your prospective donor, "I'd like to get your opinion on why these donors lose touch." You'll be blown away by their responses. During the weakness question, talk about typical problems that donors have, such as not enough time, too many organizations to support, etc., and end by using the statement, "you probably don't run into these types of problems."

When you get to the next step (opportunity section) ask them what they see the local NFP community needing and listen to their opinion – they will give it and you'll learn some important aspects of their beliefs and reasons they give.

Finally, you get to the perceived dangers and here is where you talk about fears and concerns. Are they overwhelmed with the number of "asks" they receive on a daily, weekly, monthly basis? How can you better communicate with them especially with so much mind traffic out there?

Trust comes down to the things you do, asking great questions and listening to the answers. This shows your beliefs and your actions make the prospective investor comfortable, confident and open. The more trust they have the more they give. One skill that helps create trust is found in **Element 15, Start Reading Minds.**

element

5: Start Reading Minds

"YOU REALLY READ THAT GUY WELL," AN EMPLOYEE SAID TO ME AS we left an initial meeting. We had just closed on a six figure technology project and my employee had noticed how it seemed as if I'd read the prospects mind. Well, I did, sort-of – I used my NLP training to understand what the prospect was thinking and what direction he was headed. I'm not an expert in this field, but I've studied it enough to feel comfortable showing you how to use it. In fact, I've used my knowledge and awareness to mirror and match prospective investors and help them connect to my purpose.

As described in Strategy 1, NLP is an acronym for the three most influential components tied in producing human experiences/emotions – neurology, language, and programming. According to the web definition, the neurological system regulates how our bodies function; language determines the kinds of models of the world we create. NLP programming describes the interaction between the mind and language affects the body and behavior. This process helps you understand someone when their words are either not clear or perhaps misleading. For example, you might tell the sales associate that you're interested in purchasing something in a retail store, but your body is facing the door with a facial expression making you look like you need to go to the restroom (providing different signals).

On the other hand, there are times when you connect with another person right from the second you meet them. It is almost like you've known them your entire life. The more you understand how NLP works within your own behavioral preferences, the faster your comfort level grows in identifying others preferences.

One of the most common behavioral style indicators is the DISC personality assessment. It is the most common used assessment in the sales world, improving the way people interact with each other. DISC stands for the four quadrant behavioral model based on William Moulton Marston's work[11] and demonstrates different behavior styles that we all possess. Marston examined individual behavior in the personal environments and within certain situations.

The assessment classifies four aspects of behavior by testing a person's association to certain words. The acronym means:

Dominance (D's) – relates to power, control, and assertiveness

---

[11] http://www.discprofile.com/williammoultonmarston.htm

Influence (I's) – relates to social situations and communication

Steadiness (S's) – relates to patience, persistence, and thoughtfulness

Conscientiousness (compliance) (C's) –relates to structure and organization

We each tend to emphasize one or two of the styles and incorporate all of them into our overall behavior. For example, you might be 50% D, 30% I, 5% S, and 15% C. D's tend to be intense and active when dealing with challenges. In fact, they can be described as demanding, forceful, strong, determined, and pioneering. Whereas, I's tend to influence others with charm, described as convincing, magnetic, enthusiastic, persuasive, warm, trusting, and optimistic.

When describing S's, words like steady, secure, and predicable come to mind. These people are loyal, related, deliberate, and stable. On the other hand, the last group, C's, adhere to rules and regulations. They like structure along with interaction that is careful, neat, accurate, and tactful.

In my academy, I teach NPO leaders to first understand the core fundamentals of the four styles, next to identify them in others, and then to mirror and match the style. The better you get at reading people the more your fundraising contribution will increase. When you are dealing with a D, especially a high D for example, you should be brief and to the point. They like answers and results and don't need all the facts. In fact, when you learn how to notice these characteristics in others and then customize your discussion to their preferences, you'll find your donations and sponsors significantly increase and it will seem like you're reading people's minds. This skill comes in handy as you begin Strategy 4, Flare, Flash, Burst.

Summary

- ☐ Change your attitude and terminology
- ☐ Understand how Investors think and act,
- ☐ Increase trust through your actions rather than your words
- ☐ A great commercial opens doors
- ☐ Develop your pink cat
- ☐ Create the correct investor profile so your interacting with the right people at the right time
- ☐ Key questions that often do not get asked
- ☐ Identify who is not giving to you but should

Key Action Steps

(You Can Do This Right Now):

1. Take an initial shot at creating your sizzling 59 second commercial

Part 1: _____

Part 2: _____

Part 3: _____

2. What makes you a pink cat?

_____

Tool:
*Developing a Great 59 Second Commercial

*Available at HowGoodBecomeGreat.com

strategy

4. Flare, Flash, Burst

"Sometimes our candle goes out, but is blown into flame by an encounter with another human being."
— Albert Schweitzer, Humanitarian

YOU ACCOMPLISH GREAT GOALS WHEN OTHERS PERCEIVE YOU AS genuine and provide you with the right information at the right time because your habits are authentic and credible. You can find the right decision makers by using the right questioning techniques along with harnessing the law of attraction. You attract what you are and think about rather than what you do. The reality is that investors need you to help them through the decision process while they provide the guide for you to follow to close on more funding. Remember to leverage the POWER of your board of directors and track individual contribution so you can improve on what is working and stop ineffective activities.

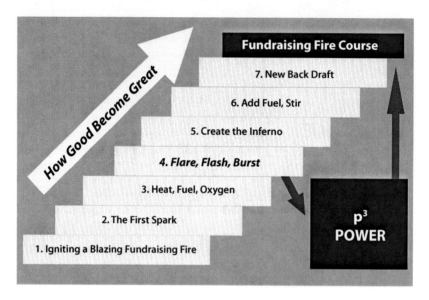

element

16: Genuine Credibility

"IF YOU WANT MORE REFERRALS THEN SIMPLY SAY PLEASE AND thank you every chance you get," the instructor said at an entrepreneurs work shop I was attending. The words were so simple, yet I knew at times I had forgotten the importance of being polite and treating every person during every interaction with the upmost respect. We often get caught in an ego battle of who achieves what. If you want to hit new fundraising levels, then you have to start with the most critical and easiest strategy you can implement today – Genuine Credibility©.

Genuine Credibility© refers to having habits that others appreciate, watch, and often emulate. This means people you come in contact with on a daily basis or connect via your personal network, appreciate and respect you at such a high level that they're willing to do or help with anything you are passionate about. They'll move mountains for you. Indeed they believe in you to the point of wanting more success for you than they do for them self. In fact, they are your cheerleader, referring you to key contacts and expanding your opportunities. Subsequently, they open up their rolodexes & databases to you, helping make critical introductions for you by not just providing names but actually making phone calls and attending meetings with you to make sure you get connected to the right people.

Credibility increases your fundraising when you foster five key habits all built around authenticity. Authenticity is defined as not false, real, and genuine. When you are authentic, you demonstrate trust and reliability through facts of action. You have habits that are evident, consistent, and create trust. People are watching what you do more than what you say.

These habits cross over industry and specialty lines and have survived for thousands of years, yet are often the most overlooked skills that one can improve. If done well, you will receive more referrals, have e-mails forwarded on to thousands of contacts, and begin to see others moving mountains for you. However, if you take these habits for granted, your efforts will result in frustration and disappointment.

People with these habits are honest, sensitive to and tolerate other views. They are friendly, patient, and responsive. They make others feel great by listening and valuing their feedback.

The Five Critical Genuine Credibility© habits include:

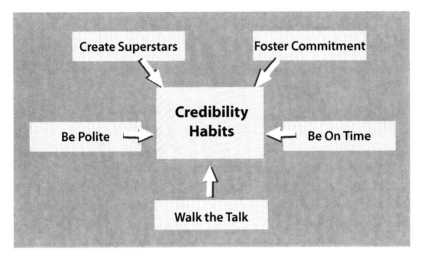

1. **Always being Polite**

   They always say please and thank you no matter the situation or environment, opening doors for others, completing proper introductions, listening while others speak, and following the proper social protocol for all interaction.

2. **Create Superstars**

   They make everyone around them look and feel important; creating opportunities for others. They don't talk negatively to other staff members or volunteers about anyone for any reason.

3. **Completing what you commit to**

   They finish what they started; making sure that if they commit to the goal or project, they get it completed. They under promise and over deliver

4. **Being on time**

   They are on time (or even early), becoming such a fixture at events and activities that others would call 911 if they failed to show up on time.

5.   **Walking the talk**

They don't just talk about it, they do it or in other words they go beyond talking the talk and they walk the walk; leading as a role model and speaking through actions rather than just words.

These habits seem very simple and anyone with common sense should know them. However, if they are not top of mind, then they become lost from your busy days filled with too much to do and not enough time to do it. When you are genuine and credible you have common decency towards others, enabling positive human connections. People want to work with and help you.

Genuine Creditability© tactics separate you from the pack, enabling you to hit new and exciting levels of personal fundraising contribution and these skills help you in your questioning process. Others will open up to you if you use the techniques discussed in **Element 17, Call 911 or Use 411**.

Call 911 or Use 411

"MY BOSS TELLS ME THAT WE CANNOT SPONSOR YOUR POLO EVENT this year," and my stomach went to my throat because I'd just realized my mistake. I had not been presenting to and negotiating with the decision maker. They did not have the authority or power to say yes. This was a fatal mistake that had cost me time, resources and money. I've seen this mistake happen more than once to NPO leaders and entrepreneurs during their fundraising roles of both the for-profit and nonprofit worlds. You end up pitching, selling, and offering opportunities to people that lack the authority to make decisions. You often articulate your value and mission well, but the person on the other side is unable to pull the trigger or move the relationship forward. They love what you are doing, your cause, and you personally but they lack the authority to approve or write the check. You find yourself calling 911 in panic over your easily avoided mistake.

The key here is to ask the right questions at the right time to reveal the decision maker without making your contact feel uncomfortable or alarmed. If done correctly, this process is like calling 411 for information because it is simple, quick, and efficient and enables you to identify the person who can write you a check.

As you go through your questioning process, you'll need to identify who is in control of the decision process. Your prospective investor must feel in control even if they have a committee or superior involved. If they feel like you're going around or above them, then they'll suffocate your actions and kill the deal quickly.

Each interaction will be different with some decisions made by one person in five minutes and others requiring several subcommittees working together over several months. This process works for donations, sponsors and grant applications. No matter which decision process they use, your only concern is identifying it early on in your process and then getting an answer (hopefully Yes) from everyone involved.

There are certain steps and techniques you use to identify which process they use, who the decision maker is, and start before you ever make contact. These steps become critical as you complete your investigation. Start with a few assumptions about the company or prospective donors based on your database and titles. For example, in the corporate structure, the Marketing Director, Community Relations, and/or Business Development may be your contact. As you may notice, I used the words "may be" because until you start the questioning process, you won't know if they are the decision maker and in some firms, the office manager has more power than the President or the IT staff has more influence on sponsorships than the Marketing Department.

There are several subscription sources that can be purchased to identify the name and contact information of the key decision makers if a business is your target. In addition, there are several web based systems for identifying key donors. These are list services containing valuable information, however they often cost money. Google is of course the obvious free tool, but a more valuable tool is LinkedIn. If you understand how to use LinkedIn properly, you identify the decision maker or find the right person who can offer and introduce you to them.

You'll need to make sure your lead tracker list identifies the decision maker, keeping your most recent correspondence organized helps you feel more comfortable and confident in your approach. In our academy, I teach NPO executives how to identify the decision maker even if you've exhausted all your search tools.

You need to understand that it may take several attempts to identify who you should be talking with regard to potential investors, whether they are donors or sponsors. The statistics show that 45% to 50% of fundraising professionals give up after making only one attempt to make contact with a prospect. It may take three, five, seven or more tries before you get to the right person but keep pushing forward. The key is to make sure you're contacting the right person before you use up valuable time and resources to make multiply attempts.

After you've identified the person you think you should be talking to and you've reached out and made contact, you'll need to verify their authority (power). This is the critical step because if you assume they have the authority and control to make crucial decisions and they don't, you'll find yourself feeling like I did at the beginning of this element, frustrated from lost time and efforts.

There are several questions and techniques for verifying your contacts authority. For example, one powerful question is, "I find that when I'm working with a potential investor (donor/sponsor), they often rely on key personnel/ their husband/wife (if it is an individual)/a committee to help them confirm relationships, but that might not be the situation with you?" Make sure you ask a question like this in an open-ended format. This one question can gently help you identify whether you're dealing with a contact that can write the check or whether you'll need to help them bring the other key decision makers into the discussion. Their answer will direct you to your next step and in many cases, you are helping them make a more educated, positive decision and overcome their fears of making a bad choice. Besides, remember people fear making serious decisions. Walter Kaufmann at Princeton[12] University in 1973 proclaimed Decidophobia as a new kind of fear of making important decisions. Kaufmann found that people would either avoid (hide) or go along to get along when put in the uncomfortable decision making situation.

In the P^3 part of the fundraising formula, power is a major step in the process. If you identify the power source while keeping the prospect in control, then you will be seen as a professional NPO leader and not just someone caught in the Borrower Phenomenon. One tool you can use to attract the targeted decision makers to your organization is **Element 18, The Law of Attraction**.

---

[12] Leadership Decision Making, Professor Hossein Arsham

18: Using the Law of Attraction

ACCORDING TO NAPOLEON HILL, ""OUR JOB AS HUMANS IS TO HOLD on to the thoughts of what we want, make it absolutely clear in our minds what we want, and from that we start to invoke one of the greatest laws in the Universe, and that's the law of attraction. You become what you think about most, but you also attract what you think about most." Hill's statement connects to your activities as an officer because you must attract the right people, resources, partners, and funding to your organization. The techniques are external, but the attraction comes from within.

By now you've all seen or at least heard of the movie "The Secret", Rhonda Burden's unique approach to teaching one of the critical steps in the foundation of life success. She points out that the law of attraction is the belief that people, opportunities, money, and resources are attracted to you because of the way you believe, think, and act.

I first learned about the law of attraction when I read Think and Grow Rich, by Napoleon Hill during college. As an Entrepreneur and nonprofit volunteer, it has guided every decision and action I've taken over the past 20 years. You'll find that your life and fundraising improve as you increase your understanding of the law and the actions you can take within its guidelines. For example, if you believe you can only fundraise $100,000 per year and your thoughts and scripts tie to that amount, then you will only attract opportunities/investors into your life that equal $100K per year.

The reality is many NPOs who seem to hit a ceiling on their efforts will find that their thoughts both individually and collectively, as well as their actions, are limiting their results. They're stuck at the donation threshold, raising the same amounts (+ or minus 3%) year after year. The threshold is the top amount of funds that can be brought in by your contacts and network. In other words, you may need to break into new networks with higher income individuals or larger corporate coffers.

If your vision is to raise a $10,000,000 this year then you must attract into your life people, opportunities, and resources that have the capacity to bring you this level of fundraising. If you do not make changes or utilize the law of attraction, your chances of hitting larger fundraising goals diminishes.

The first questions to address are both internal and external and will begin the process of attracting to you the relationships and resources you need to grow. Questions like "What do I know about myself? "Who do I know right now? And "Who do I need to know?" I recently sat with a very successful entrepreneur, who has creating hundreds of amazing relationships over the last 45 years. He founded a very successful magazine with a well known brand and since that starting point he's created a network of people who are the "who's who" in the U.S. and Europe, including Fortune 500 CEO's, the top of the Forbes list, key politicians, and on and on. My ongoing experience with him has taught me that you attract people into your life by what you're like both on the inside and outside which includes your values, vision, friends, influences, beliefs, and habits.

How do you answer the first question – What do I know about myself? It might help to write out the following sentence, "I know I am_____ (fill in the blank). You can fill in the space with words such as: smart, successful, giving, kind, helpful, dynamic, powerful, influential, inspired, etc. Each word has power and connects you to a new relationship. As you continue to answer the other questions you'll find that a profile begins to develop as to who you are and who you can attract into your life as well as the NPO you represent. The key is to attract people and resources that make a difference and not just a small difference but a major impact.

The key obstacle becomes attracting the right resources at the right time. As children, we're taught that our imagination is important with no limitations or boundaries. As adults we're conditioned to be "realistic" and to take our "heads out of the clouds". Does your board or supporters say to you? "That's not a realistic goal for an NPO this size." Or "We've never raised that type of money."

Great NPOs are lead by positive, optimistic people who tend to attract other happy, great people and resources. Happy people tend to be happy because they're living the life they wanted to live. They're living their dreams and attracting the right resources to their organization when the resources are required. They focus their mind on what they want and then take action to accomplish their dreams. They avoid focusing on what they do not want, attracting the same type of positive investors and resources that other successful, growing NPOs attract.

Attracting great investors to your NPO starts with not only who you attract, but your ability to bring out their POWER which I cover in **Element 19, Harness Your Board POWER**.

element

19: Harness Your Board POWER

"WATCH HOW THE WOOD STARTS TO CHANGE COLOR BEFORE YOU see the flame," my father said to me as I watched one of his many experiments. He looked like Mr. Hyde turning into Doctor Jackal as the words shot from his mouth. On this day he was heating a 2x4 to show (and analyze) how material begins to change color and form before you actually see the red hot flame. The wood actually goes through a significant process that the human eye is unable to detect (because it happens so quickly). It's been several years since I witnessed his many experiments but I never did forget lesson in it and have since taken it with me into the NPO world. It reminds me of all the little things; the preparation, work, and behind the scenes activities that must take place in order to heat up your fundraising ability of your Board Directors and get their activities on fire.

The word Power in the Fundraising formula has a duel meaning, deciphering authority/decision making and leveraging the Power of your partners, clients, volunteers, and staff for fundraising purposes. However, your most critical POWER partner is your board.

Having a powerful board is not about operations or governance; both are very important, however it's about the power of your board to raise money either through direct actions or the actions of their networks, vendors, resources and strategic partners (Power Partners). If the number one priority of your board is to help you raise money, then you need to make fundraising the number one focus. Like the sun darting into a room, the tone of meetings, direction of agendas, and even the words you use should beam to the members that fundraising is not only important but expected. This is your chance to change the culture and make it a fun process for everyone. You can do this in a very positive way.

The problem with igniting the board member efforts is gauging their abilities to execute the plans and tools you deliver. In many cases, a board member does not have direct resources to allow him / her to write you specific checks or he / she may not have a very deep personal network. However, the member is passionate about you and your cause so you need to provide tools and processes that make their life easier. Focus on the POWER process.

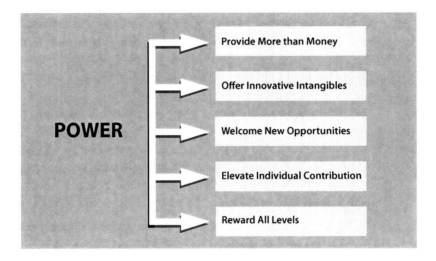

POWER is about expanding your influence and creating new fundraising results for the organization.

P P stands for Provide More Than Money. Even though the number one priority of your board is to provide funding to the NPO whether directly from them or sources in their circle of influence, you need them to provide more than money in order to make changes and accomplish more significant milestones. This value is critical, often hard to define, and makes the difference between success and failure. Through self analysis, simple changes, and authenticity, they will begin to manage time differently, create positive case studies, and re-write old money scripts. We need to understand, and if necessary, change their mind set about fundraising.

O O stands for Offering Innovative Intangibles. An intangible is not always clear to define or perceived by the sense of touch. These are things that often cannot be picked up or they may be hard to value. In fact, in order to get your arms around it, you may have to see how each individual board member's efforts connect to the overall mission and fundraising goals. Examples of intangibles include customer good will, aesthetic appeal or team morale. For our purposes, I'm using the term to mean steps you can have members take or gifts they can offer that go beyond tangible items such as dollars and checks. The reality is that if they can master the things not seen or held, they can reach new, increased fundraising goals. Furthermore, intangibles take on a more difficult process when expressing them in an individual or board structure and understanding which ones affect performance. They are often identified with a board's overall results whether they are positive or negative. The NPO they represent is looking for them to offer more in the way of collaboration, knowledge, processes, and relationships, but you might have problems articulating your needs or how to put them on the path to reaching those goals. Great training can do this.

W W stands for Welcome New Opportunities. When you welcome new opportunities, you set the stage for your board to grow and develop new revenue channels. Who have the members not contacted to ask for funds? According to Boardsource, only 40% of the board members in the country are comfortable with asking for donations (probably more like 70% to 80%). They are often uncomfortable because they haven't been taught how to properly ask or they continue to go down the same road. In fact, members often farm the same list and people and the natural progression is for that list to get smaller and smaller every six months. I'm defining "unique" as the only one or the sole example, leading to the improbable. Members may have opportunities that have are unparallel to previous efforts whether they be people they have not talked to about your NPO or resources they've overlooked. There are individual contribution results waiting for you to accomplish.

E E stands for Elevate. We are often asked to take our contributions to the "next level" but next level means different things to different people. The key here is to focus on small shifts, keeping in mind the value of improvement over perfection. Evaluate the details of what is being asked of your board and if they understand the NPO's expectations. If they do understand the expectations, you can start to elevate each individual's own contributions. Elevate means to rise to a higher place or state, promoting the overall fundraising objectives not once a month or quarter, but in every interaction. This is not about being a cheerleader. Rather, it is about using enthusiasm and tools to motivate yourself and your fellow board members to raise the bar, expect something better, and know that they have support and resources to fall back on.

R R stands for Reward All Levels. Donors, sponsors, cheerleaders and superstars love appreciation and while some like cash and prizes others go for fame and portfolio bullet points. The key here is to reward everyone at every level. It is often as simple as saying thank you or sending a hand written note each and every time there is an opportunity. In other cases, they may need to send a gift certificate or tickets to an event. Either way, you must help them connect to every contact that helps or even attempts to help the NPO. To further state this point, appreciate and thank everyone all the time, every minute, every second. This is a simple concept, but overlooked again and again.

I've sat on many Board of Directors both in the not-for-profit and for-profit world over the last 15 years and been fortunate to see the good, the bad and the ugly. One thing I continued to see over and over was the lack of contribution that most board members make when it comes to raising money. I'm not referring to the boards that require a minimum donation (ex: $5,000 to be on the board), although many times this minimum is set too low. Most board members want to help, have the passion in their heart to make a difference, and are willing to learn, however the problem is that the NPO does not have a process in place to help the member help themselves. The volunteers already have a ton of commitments so they get caught in the NPO time trap or they have a large network and the Giving Trap becomes a problem.

There are hundreds of systems, software, and books out there. The challenge is implementing one that fits your organization's unique needs, challenges, and goals. Lets' face it, your board is made up of volunteers with very little incentives other than "doing nice things," and "making the world a better place," which are great, impactful themes, but fall short on motivating people and changing behavior.

In my How Good Board Members Become Great Fundraisers Workshop (available via webinar), we take board of directors through the five components of POWER, unleashing their ability to overcome the 7 key challenges and make a difference. Their power is not about the checks they write, but the checks and value that come from their network, relationships, and personal activities. Also, I cover these assumed challenges and 25 tactics to help overcome them in the book version.

As an NPO leader, one of the best tools you can implement is the SPARK Drill. The entire board can increase contributions by utilizing this drill which, when implemented, correctly helps leadership ask key questions and improve the team moral while at the same time help each individual break through the knowledge ceiling. I'm not talking about a raw raw session with Anthony Robbins in front of the room, although that wouldn't hurt. I am referring to a quick, outlined approach that leads to 50%, 100%, 1000% increases in activities. The challenge is to do this with a simple method that is not time consuming or disorganized. If you are part of the internal leadership or an organization that doesn't currently use a method of this nature, using this tool at your next board or committee meeting could be valuable. Of course, fundraising cannot take up all or a significant part of the meetings, but it can have impact if delivered appropriately. Anticipate about 12 to 15 minutes covering all five sections. It's time to light the first SPARK.

After this tool is implemented you will see members improve their efforts by 500% in some cases – the results will beat your expectations. However, you must have a tracking system, **Element 20, Tracking Contribution Levels**, in order to see what tools and processes are working and which ones are failing.

Utilize the SPARK drill

Situation

- Review the overall NPO Fundraising Goal & Have each board member pull out their Goal Card

- Have each member very quickly go around the table to say how close % wise they are to hitting their own personal fundraising goal

- Time - 3 minutes

 **Positive**

- Have one board member share their own personal fundraising success story
- If no one volunteers be prepared with your own
- Time - 3 minutes

 **Approach**

- Go over one technique that can help – i.e. fundraising time block, 60 second commercial, negative reverse, avoid the giving trap, etc.
- Take one question on the technique
- Time - 3 minutes

 **Reward**

- Review one idea of how to say thank you or show appreciation to someone who has donated, sponsored, or assisted in some way
- Provide a reward to a member who did something unique, told a great success story, or signed on a key sponsor, etc.
- Time - 3 minutes

 **Knowledge**

- Provide one quick fact or statistic they didn't know about fundraising and/or the NPO world – make it interesting and not necessarily pulling on the heart strings.
- Time - 3 minutes

20: Tracking Contribution Levels

"AND THE TOP FUNDRAISER FOR THIS YEAR IS,..." THE FOUNDATION President said my name at the end of his statement at our annual awards banquet. I was excited and pleased to have that honor for the fifth year in a row and accomplishing it for a group of volunteers that were incredible fundraisers. It was a team effort built on individual actions. Each year we tracked the fundraising contributions of all our members and board. This included both the checks they wrote and the value (in kind contributions) that came in from their relationships (cash for auction items, sponsorship dollars, direct donations). This award made me see the importance of tracking individual contribution at all levels of your organization so you can understand where the money is coming from and implement techniques and strategies that work while unloading those that do not. It doesn't have to deal with creating competition or stroking egos because if done correctly it can motivate and unit. In fact, if you do not have a method for tracking, then making adjustments and improvements is practically impossible.

As part of my three year strategic plan while leading the foundation, I helped create a tracking tool for individual contributions. This tool helps identify how an investor gets involved and who is their contact. The process works with your accounting system (especially QuickBooks and Black Baud CRM), providing methods to identify the sources without hurting feelings or causing people to get upset. And you don't have to worry about fights over contacts or firms because you simply split the contribution. In fact, you can identify internal staff, volunteers, board members, and even clients who are initiating opportunities for you and provide simple lists of recent investors to your board and volunteers.

We offer a contribution tracker form/system to our clients to make it easy to get started. This system includes identifying the marketing source and the person who created the relationship in the first place. If you can master this step, then you will have feedback that can help adjust your process when you're not getting the expected results. It will also help you identify and intensively implement tactics that are working while ending ineffective ones. However, if you do not track contributions, then you miss opportunities to say thank you or show proper appreciation for the people out in the community making a big difference for your group. In the end understanding the people and resources helping you move forward helps create the Inferno in Strategy 5.

Strategy 4 Summary

- ⊟ Genuine Credibility Habits help form great relationships

- ⊟ Using a questioning system to identify key decision makers saves you time and headaches

- ⊟ Defining what a fundraising board looks like

- ⊟ Help the board provide more than money

- ⊟ Increase the intangibles

- ⊟ Unique ways to increase the money that each board member raises

- ⊟ Ideas for rewards

Key Action Steps
(You Can Do This Right Now):

1. List one question you can use to confirm that you're dealing with the right decision maker

   _____

2. Which Genuine Credibility Habit do you need to work on right now?

   _____

Tool:
*SPARK Drill Form

*Available at HowGoodBecomeGreat.com

strategy

5: Create the Inferno

YOU NEED TO COME ACROSS TO ALL CURRENT AND POTENTIAL investors as a professional who understands their industry, value, and ROI, avoiding the Borrower Phenomenon. You're not asking for a donation or sponsorship, you are providing value in return for an investment. They must see you as a vital part of their mission and/or community contribution; not just another donation. Furthermore, you and your organization can bring out your exceptional ability in each and every interaction, providing solutions and opportunities. Now, you are on the verge of creating an amazing Investor (fundraising/business) Development Plan to go along with your NPO's strategic, marketing, web, cultivation, and other action plans. Finally, you need to fill up your pipeline with qualified investors (donors, sponsors, in-kind trade), managing your time differently and as efficiently as possible.

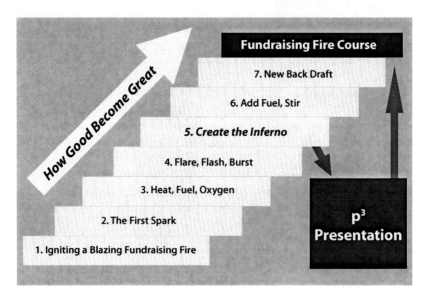

element

21: Put On Your Solution Hat

"I THINK YOU HAVE SOME INDIGESTION ISSUES," THE DOCTOR TOLD me as our appointment ended. As I listened to his recommendation or diagnosis, I realized how similar the process is for a doctor to work with a patient as it is for an NPO DD or ED to work with potential investors. If you do a great job of analyzing the investor (patient), asking great questions; then you can make your recommendation (diagnosis) and help the investor (patient) make a great decision (perfect remedy). However, one the challenges that I see officers running into is selling or pitching (diagnosing) before they hear the symptoms and understand the investor's motivation, challenges, and/or concerns.

There is no doubt that a dynamic and emotional presentation works, however you must know when to put it in play.

The "understand before you recommend" approach is probably new to you because most trainers do not teach NPO professionals the pain/gain game or seek to understand before being understood (ala Steven Covey) process. They leave this component for the for-profit world overlooking how effective it can be in the NPO world.

The reality is that your potential investors donate or sponsor for their own reasons and not yours. When you put on your fundraising hat, you want to act similar to the Doctor putting on his medical jacket. You need to examine the investor, asking appropriate questions that provide you with enough feedback to make a professional recommendation (which, by the way, isn't always to give your organization money). Indeed, the prospect will respect you more as a professional if you help them make a good decision for their own gain first and you/your organization second. You're looking for a match at this point, matching their needs and challenges with your NPO offering. It can be hard to turn away an investor, but in the long run you'll raise more money than you ever have before. Besides, strong arming or using aggressive sales tactics to get a sponsor can have horrible future ramifications.

If you do a good job during the questioning phase of your process, then you'll have the opportunity to match your solutions (NPO offerings) to their pain or gain. The questions you'll be providing matches to include:

- Are there any nonprofit sectors you're passionate about – i.e. dogs, kids, environment, grandparents?
- What types of organizations do you give your time or money to?
- What do you look for in NPOs?
- How do you know you've made a great investment?

- How much money do you typically give each year? (Budget & Investment Questions)

- Who do you know that might want to help our group?

- When was the last time you did a sponsorship where you felt you received 10x the value as the cost of the sponsorship?

- Where do you think our community is falling down?

These are just a few example questions that help set up the presentation part of your process. Your intent is to ask engaging questions to gather enough objective information and emotional keys to deliver a recommendation to your prospect focused on their individual fears and opportunities and your organizational fit.

There are plenty of books on organizing PowerPoint presentations and providing the right materials and / or proposals so for this book, I'm just focusing on your process; when to present and how to match their issues to your value. You need to focus on connecting your benefits to their concerns, desires, future plans, and opportunities. This is your opportunity to match the key parts of your NPO offering or value during the presentation phase to each of the identified investor issues.

At the point when you understand their concerns, gains, authority level and budget limitations, you'll want to present your solutions. Again, the process is still focused on them. For example, if they talk about their community concerns of lost productivity for their employees or consumer theft because of the dropout rate in the local community, you can match your organizations work with young teens and the reduction in crime that has occurred because of your efforts. This is an objective point rather than emotional. One of your tactics is to write all of your benefits in one column (easy to do this as you're questioning and taking notes) and then write their issues, ideas, challenges, passions in a second column. Now, connect each issue with your offering and make the match.

The mistake that most NPOs make is falling into the eagerness trap and pitching or diagnosing before they know the prospective investors pain or gain. For example, you tell them that your NPO has been around for 100 years, but the investor may think that means your organization is old or complacent. It's not that you hide anything; it's that you emphasize the matching solutions the same way the Doctor makes a diagnosis; asking good questions, taking notes, and then making the right recommendation. Besides, a Doctor doesn't tell you all the great things about themselves (Harvard MD, Physician of the year, Doctor for 45 years, etc.) because their focused on you. In the end, this often takes more time on your part, but builds a stronger bond with the investor or partner in the long term.

When you properly put your fundraising hat on, you rise above the pack with professionalism, differentiating you and your organization. This process is more about what you do than what you say and comes in handy when you bring out **Element 22, Exceptional Ability**.

element

22: Exceptional Ability

"DO YOU HAVE THE OPPORTUNITY TO DO WHAT YOU DO BEST EVERY day?" This quote/question comes from the StrengthsFinder 2.0 book. When I first read the book, the question hit me straight between the eyes and I wondered out loud, "Do I?" I've changed it for you to say, "Do you and your NPO have the opportunity to do what you do best every day?" One way for you to improve your fundraising levels is to fall in love with the three key parts to the process: relationships, subject passion, and prospecting. This includes identifying what you do best personally in combination with the entity's core strengths.

When you look at most successful for-profit corporations or non profits in the country, they do something exceptionally well; not trying to be all things to all people but focused on delivering one product or service better than the competition. They have an exceptional ability in the market place that positions them head and shoulders above the rest. In many cases this ability is real and tangible but in most cases the ability is more of a feeling or perceived contribution or a "brand" experience.

For example, Starbucks is known for coffee, but one of the firm's exceptional abilities is to create a meeting atmosphere like no other. You can meet at one of their 15,000 stores located in one of forty four countries and enjoy a beverage and snack. There is probably better coffee from other sources within a baseball throw of a location, but you won't find a better meeting place. Similar to Starbucks, the abilities of your NPO are as exceptional as your staff and board, but now let's figure out what those exceptional abilities are and ways to bring them out when interacting with investors.

Begin with your organization and your clientele. You know who you help from a 10,000 foot view, but what one thing makes your organization different from the others? For example, if you help homeless people or families, your exceptional ability might be handing them a positive card each day with a simple inspirational saying on it. Your investor makes investments in one or more NPOs because they have a great relationship and they can see and understand the unique value that organization delivers. This is where you tie their ROI to your clientele, creating a bond that is both emotionally and objectively based.

Next, take a look at yourself and evaluate the strength assessment results you identified in Strategy 2 (Find Your Strength). Let's break down the themes identified in the Strengthsfinder book, evaluate your top 5 themes, and figure out how they connect to your unique talents.

List out your five themes below

———————————————————

———————————————————

———————————————————

———————————————————

———————————————————

The Gallop group interviewed over 1.5 million people to quantify the 34 distant attributes or "personal themes," which : achiever, activator, adaptability, analytical, arranger, belief, command, communication, competition, connectedness, consistency, context, deliberative, discipline, empathy, focus, futuristic, harmony, ideation, and include individualization, input, intellect, learner, maximization, positivity, relater, responsibility, restorative, self-assurance, significance, strategic, and woo. When you understand which five are your top themes and how they affect your day-to-day activities, you'll begin to improve your fundraising efforts.

Your results may help you conclude that you're in the wrong position or they may improve the way you interact with the people you need to interact with on a daily basis. This is your chance to improve your prospecting, questioning, and presenting skills while mirroring and matching the prospective investor's traits and style.

Another way to identify your exceptional ability is to confirm which parts of the prospecting game you enjoy. Typically it comes to four areas including: hunting, maintaining, farming, or maximizing.

When you are a hunter your passion is identifying potential investors, finding them, and the thrill of the first interaction. You enjoy starting fresh each day and overcoming the usual obstacles that you run into each and every time. Once you have the deal closed (obtained the hunted), then you move onto the next prospect.

When you are a maintainer, you like taking over the process once the prospect becomes a serious prospect. You enjoy answering their questions and making them feel comfortable with their investment decision. Once the ice is broken you feel comfortable moving ahead, exploring and understanding their reasons.

The farmer is an NPO leader who likes fostering and cultivating relationships. Similar to a farmer, you enjoy planting the seeds of the new relationship, putting water on them (consistent communication), and watching things grow (bringing in more dollars as the years pass).

The maximizing part reflects a person that focuses on making everything in the relationship better and constantly providing new and improved value to the investor. They never need to ask for anything because you are already providing it, always one step ahead.

As you may have noticed, all four areas are part of your process in fundraising, however, if you identify which one is your strength (exceptional ability), you can either delegate the other steps, find technology to help fill in the gap, or outsource to an individual or firm specializing in an area you've identified as weak.

As an NPO leader, the exceptional abilities of both you and your organization become a key to developing new investors, keeping the ones you have, and running a professional process. Potential investors and partners can feel, not just see, when you're using your exceptional ability. You end up bringing out your passion in an authentic way and providing a rope for your contacts to pull you to your fundraising goals. After you've identified your exceptional ability, you need to put **Element 23, Investor Development Plan,** into action.

element

23: The 7 Second Investor Development Plan

"WE NEED A $50,000 TITLE SPONSOR FOR OUR EVENT," THE POLO chair told the board during a key meeting. I simply looked at them and said, "Great, let's go find them." Although my answer was optimistic and I'm sure a few eye brows went up, we still had to create a strategy and tactics to make it happen. It came down to having a great business development plan focused on utilizing volunteers, key relationships, and ideal investors. This is a similar process to the for-profit world and should be taken very seriously.

In the for-profit environment you typically form a business development or sales plan in order to accomplish revenue goals. So for the NPO world, you need a simple, straight-forward Investor Development Plan or Fundraising Plan. This plan consists of 7 steps including:

Step 1: Outline the NPO Fundraising Yearly Objectives

- ▣ Summarize the key goals and objectives of the organization, including goals under all the other categories like governance, marketing, client services, etc. and then connect each goal or category to the fundraising efforts of the organization.

- ▣ Provide incentives and a path for the internal staff to see how accomplishing a fundraising goal leads to more opportunities in other areas (i.e. more clients served).

- ▣ Review your average cost of client served (i.e. $100 equals one client) and compare to average fundraising dollar.

Step 2: Establish Development Director / ED / Officers Personal Fundraising Goal (Card and breakout plan)

- ▣ Identify personal fundraising goals; breaking it down into the three key areas: donors, sponsors, and in-kind trade (power partners). As I've discussed throughout the book, these investors can provide value in many different ways.

- ▣ Make passive grants a separate category so you do not dilute your other numbers.

- ▣ Put all your goals in writing including behavior ones like number of contacts per week, number of dials, number of e-mails, etc.

- ▣ Use a goal card (carry it with you) to keep a constant reminder of what you're shooting for and the meaning to the organization for obtaining it.

Step 3: Narrow down the Ideal & Segmented Investors

- Highlight the targeted ideal investor (Strategy 3)
- Write the ideal investor description with all the demographics and psychographics you identified in that strategy. This helps you understand your target contact and could mean multiple descriptions if, for example, your ideal sponsor is different than the donors.

Step 4: Identify key strategic partners (Power Partners)

- Identify which in-kind/strategic partners (POWER Partners) will benefit your NPO the most.
- Create resellers (call them POWER Partners in the NPO world). These are partners who deliver value via trade, referrals, introductions, and other key resources. In fact, NPOs often turn away opportunities because they do not know how to monetize certain products/goods that many vendors can provide (creativity become a great skill here).

Step 5: Develop Daily, Weekly, Monthly Behavior

- Detail the daily behavior you confirmed in step 2.
- Write out your year, quarter, month and week. The more detailed analysis you complete at this point, the more likely you are to reach your individual goals.

Step 6: Measure and Monitor

- Understand how you'll track the revenue and behavior goals including the tools and software (spreadsheets versus software)

- Add in your close ratios (i.e. how many dials, meet-ings, e-mails, etc. does it take for you to close an investors. Do one ration for each category (major donors, sponsors, trade)

- Examine how you will account for successes and chal-lenges (failed attempts).

Step 7: Create an Adjustment System

- Make sure you have a method and process to evalu-ate results and then make adjustments.

- Clearly define, "What does success look like for me and our NPO?" This helps you identify how you will know the process is not working (monitoring) and when to make adjustments.

This Investor Development Plan is simple and takes only a few minutes to fill outline and a few hours to complete, but will be incredibly important for you in reaching new and higher fundraising goals. If you clearly define your action plan for this year (in a short and simple fashion), then you're well on your way to avoiding **Element 24, The NPO Time Trap**.

element

24: Avoiding the NPO Time Trap

"OUR DEVELOPMENT OFFICER SPENDS TIME ON GRANT APPLICA-tions and fostering donors," was the answer from an NPO executive I was meeting with when I asked about their Development Director's daily activities. I was trying to get a feel for what their actual day looked like and where they could be misusing their time.

Officers in nonprofits are no different than anyone else in the business world because they struggle with how to organize their time to accomplish key priorities. The problem is heighted by the many roles they have to take on because of lack of budget and resources. They wear many hates and end up spending too much time on low priority activities.

It is hard to find a person in the country who would not admit to struggling with time management or the additional responsibilities brought on by adding more commitments. You end up caught in the NPO time trap because you do not use a time system customized for fundraising activities (Prospecting). You end up spending your days on tasks and projects that are good for the organization but not beneficial to bringing in more revenue (funds). In fact, according to Dan Sullivan from the Strategic Coach Program, "Most people work in a time and effort economy, where they organize their lives according to bureaucratic strategies. These strategies, for the most part, require time and effort but do not produce results." You want the limited time you have spent on the most productive tactics that bring about the best possible results.

You need a new strategy since we are all trying to do more in less time. In my book, *How Good Board Members Become Great Fundraisers*, I discuss a simple process for board members to carve out 15 to 30 minutes each week to do fundraising. As an NPO Director, your task is to target 4 to 5 hours per day initially on investor development priorities. According to Doug Morrow from Trusted Counsel [13], a Development Offer should possess six key skills with the most important ones being high ethical standards and self initiation. I would add to his list ability to spend time selling.

In fact, as a key officer in the entity, all of your time overlaps with each role and work category, burdening your schedule in one way or another. The idea is a dual result; focus on getting more time for fundraising activities and performing the behavior that generates the best results. Ask yourself how much time you really spend on prospecting efforts and how is that time structured? Now, track your time for one

---

[13] http://www.bizceos.com/2010/04/26/fundraising-six-crucial-qualities-to-look-for-in-a-development-officer/

to two weeks (e-mail info@billyounginspires.com for a form) and see how much time you spend on investor development activities. The statistics say you spend more time on grant applications and event planning which are important activities but seen as more passive than active.

The NPO Professional Fundraising Time System© was created to help avoid the NPO time trap and it includes two main tactics; blocking out fundraising time and connecting to the people and firms that can help your organization the most (spending time with the people who can write the largest checks).

Ralph Waldo Emerson hit the nail on the head when he said, "This time, like all times, is a very good one, if we but know what to do with it." The first step in the Fundraising Time Managemnet System is to discipline yourself to block out your calendar (either computer or paper based), dedicating a 3 to 5 hour block of time each day for completing twenty five to fifty key fundraising (prospecting) activities. This time block is just for fundraising tasks and not for other officer duties. Over time, you'll expand from three hours to six or more. Within each hour block you'll want to break it down to 30-minute chunks. You'll need to identify the block at the beginning of the month and then review and make adjustments at the beginning of each week. Friday afternoon or early Monday morning is a great time to complete the planning for the blocks or simply add this tactic into your current weekly planning procedures. Additional good times are right before or after your weekly executive/internal staff meetings because typically you are more excited and relevant information is at top of mind. The intent is to have pre-determined tasks and get more specific results in less time which creates a habit of keeping the block consistent for each day and week.

Once you've blocked the time, you'll want to write down what you anticipate working on, keeping in mind the importance of simplicity. This is your action plan for the next week and is broken out into dials, e-mails, follow ups, top 10 club, networking events, and strategic partner contacts.

The NPO Fundraising Time Management Form is a great tool for identifying these tasks, writing in bullet lists in the specific time block. It only takes about 15 to 30 minutes to complete each week and if that seems excessive then think about the saying, "failing to plan is planning to fail." For example, you might put down that you will do 20 e-mails, make 15 return phone calls, 30 warm calls, or search the web for 45 minutes to uncover a new resource or a new sponsor on Monday morning from 10:00 to 2:00. Not only write in the activities, but confirm who you will be calling or e-mailing and which potential web searches you plan to conduct. In one week if you follow this system, you will have made over 200 phone calls, 75 e-mails, and completed 3.5 hours of research. Now taking this out over a year, you'll find your fundraising numbers increasing by hundreds of percent. Remember that you'll typically find that one task equals three to five minutes of time. Lastly, customize this block to your schedule and if you have to move it, discipline yourself to keep it within that same week.

After you've confirmed your time block, the activities you define within that block must be based on your priorities and the best return for your invested time. This means using your development plan detailed in Element 23. You identified your target list based off of your ideal investor, confirmed research resources, daily behavior numbers, and key fundraising objectives of the NPO. Place those tasks within the fundraising blocks, persist and push forward, completing as many of the identified tasks as possible.

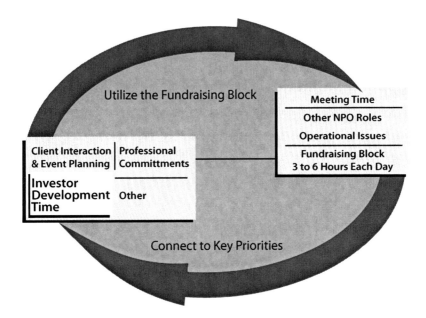

Marcia Wieder said, "It's how we spend our time here and now, that really matters. If you are fed up with the way you have come to interact with time, change it." You may have great technique and skill and even lots of years of experience, but if you manage your fundraising time poorly, you need to make a change. Improving your time management will help when you start **Strategy 6, Add Gasoline and Stir**.

Strategy 5 Summary

- Great fundraisers are great consultants, listening and helping the investor make a great decision
- Develop a detailed Investor Development Plan
- Identify key strategic partners
- Grab hold of what your NPO is really good at
- Find your personal exceptional ability
- Manage your time better and optimize your fundraising priorities and opportunities

Key Action Steps

(You Can Do This Right Now):

3. List one question you can ask that makes you look more like a Doctor than a sales person

    _____

4. What is your exceptional ability?

    _____

Tool:
*Purchase Strengthsfinder book

*Available at HowGoodBecomeGreat.com

strategy

6: Add FUEL, Stir

> *"The very existence of flame-throwers proves that some time, somewhere, someone said to themselves, You know, I want to set those people over there on fire, but I'm just not close enough to get the job done. "*

> — George Carlin

YOU NEED TO UNDERSTAND THE IMPORTANCE OF CREATING & FUELing great partnerships and relationships including initial formation, obtaining referrals, beneficial introductions, and duplicating your efforts. You want to avoid the 7 deadly sins of networking and ask for help at the right time, detail what a great introduction looks like and create and develop SuperStar and POWER supporters. People want to help you, but they must know in detail how to do it.

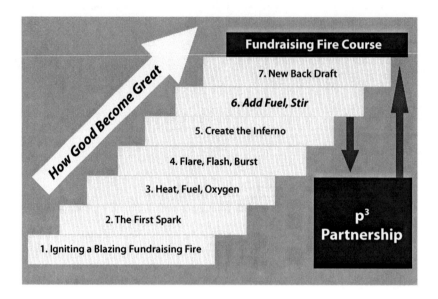

element

25: FUEL Your Relationships

"AFTER 8 YEARS I RECEIVED A REFERRAL FROM THEM." THIS STATE-ment was part of a presentation I did for a local group regarding networking and creating great relationships. I was making a point about having patience and persistence with your networks; always giving before you get. The process of relationship building is about taking a long term approach with a positive attitude. If you implement the right system you'll foster more relationships, help out more people, and achieve key fundraising objectives.

Did you ever hear the saying, "It's not what you know, but who you know that matters?" My version, which is customized for the NPO world is, "it is not who you know, but who they know and are willing to connect to you." Building relationships is tricky and it can be difficult to find a process that fits your unique talents and perspective. You want to build relationships in a step-by-step process that fits your personality in a manner that is not phony or quirky, but authentic and heart-felt. In fact, my sales coach would say, "how many people of power are you an arm's length away from?"

The reality of hitting new fundraising levels is about whom you know not what you know (I'm sure you've never heard that one). Don't misunderstand me because you need to improve your knowledge, skills, techniques, and systems but how many people in your current network can move mountains for you? Do you have 2 SuperStars or 20? The range can be the difference between raising $1,000,000 and $10,000,000.

"How do you know so many people," an NFP leader said to me earlier this year. I answered quickly and from the gut saying, "I simply try to create great relationships, provide as much value as possible, and give before I ever get anything in return." As I explained to them the process I've learned and use each day, I realized that the Add Gasoline (FUEL) and Stir chapter of this book was finished.

Relationships, as you know, are built on trust that can take many years to establish. This trust is an integral part of gaining donor's and sponsor's help and assistance. Developing the right level of trust is about evaluating and leveraging your existing circle of influence, targeting the right people in your circle, providing value before you ever receive anything and thinking long term.

The FUEL model (Diagram Follows) shows the flow of the process and goes deeper than just trustworthiness. It starts with Foster, proceeds to the understanding step, on to empowerment, and finishes with leverage. This model works in a two-fold process representing the steps in the evolution of a relationship and the levels of closeness. Each step involves evaluating your relationships and identifying which ones are most important, how to cultivate them, and ways to say good bye to the ones that do not move you forward. You grow each relationship by taking the person through the five levels of development called the C5 Formula demonstrated later in this element.

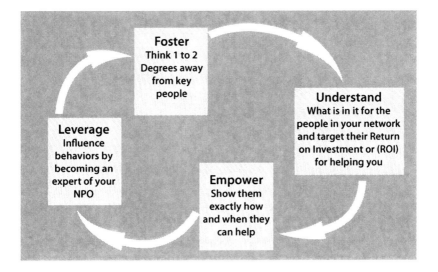

For most of us, the most important relationships are with God/Spirituality and/or Family so for my purposes here I'm not going to include those intimate relationships in the discussion. The model I use refers to current and new developing relationships and how you can guide your contacts through a process of growth.

The first step is changing or confirming your current mind set about relationships; realizing that your one to two degrees away from any person you'd like to get to know. The six degrees of separation idea, set out by Frigyes Karinthy, refers to the idea that every person on earth is at most six steps away from any other person. The growth of technology and other tools means that you're probably now one to two degrees rather than six degrees away. You want to create a list of your closest relationships to identify the degrees with the total names ranging from five to ten people (go as high as you'd like but remember the higher the quantity of names the more time and commitment required). In fact, if you only have one then we have identified your first problem, but if you have 500 then we've isolated a different type of challenge. These are strong relationships, close enough to you that you'd be comfortable calling these people for help if you were stuck on the side of the road. This is more than just you having their contact information and met with them two years ago for coffee. If your list is 15 people long, then you'll want to hand pick the top five to ten. These are relationships that are strong, but if strengthened could provide more value to your fundraising goals.

Next, you want to approach the building process with lots of patience and understanding; all the while, identifying what's in it for the person you're interacting with as you move to the next step. Examine how you can bring them value, instituting your Give to Get Formula.

When you empower people or use the E part of the FUEL formula, you show them exactly who you are, the types of referrals that benefit you, leads you're targeting, and how your contact can help you with your objectives. Indeed, you can empower these key people to aid your efforts. However, you'll want to be authentic in your approach, making sure you listen to their objectives and take a vested interest in helping them succeed.

The last step is to strengthen your leverage (but not in a negative, reinforced manor) in the relationship by becoming an outstanding expert in not only your organization but the NPO industry overall. The more they see you as an expert and professional, the more they'll want to interact with and help you. This is your chance to prove how serious you are about your role and impact. They'll open doors because they'll feel confident in your ability to interact and handle different personality types and situations. They will rest assured that you can handle the personalities of their contacts.

Relationship building is probably the number one most important skill set and use of time that a NPO Officer can obtain and use. Everyone knows this to be true, but few ever really master the process and have a system to implement that keeps them on track.

Using the FUEL process helps grow long term relationships that provide impact for both you and the other person(s). Great networking is about getting the process started and connecting with people who can help.

Here are some key questions for you at this point:

- Who are your most important relationships?
- How do you know who is most important?
- How often do you talk to them?
- How do you contact them?
- What do you know about them?
- How can you help them?

In my academy, I teach five levels of relationship building which are shown here. The model reflects the importance of having connectors (closest relationships) and then shows how an initial communication (collision) can lead by way of each step in the model to a stronger and stronger relationship. At each step, the center of Influence changes, growing from weak to strong.

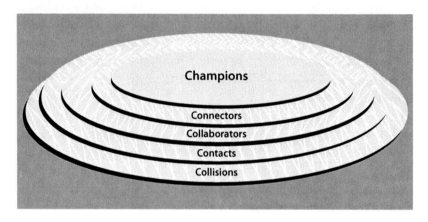

As you network and develop more relationships, you'll want to identify which phase of development you're in and understand how to move the relationship to the next level. In fact, when your developing new relationships, keep your eye on the next Element, SuperStars Improve the Party, because one powerful influencer can explode your fundraising by 1000%.

element

26: Superstars Improve the Party

"JUST PLAN TO BE AT MY OFFICE ON TUESDAY AT 2:00 AND SHAWN will be there." This was a call I received from a great champion a few years back and demonstrated to me the power of providing more than just a referral or a lead and actually participating in the connection process. My champion wasn't just making an introduction he was becoming part of my process and success. Since that day, I've focused on going the extra mile to help people get connected and in the process; I've created the idea of SuperStar supporters for all of my nonprofit activities.

In a 2009 Bank of America Study[14], Wealthy philanthropists' motivations for giving demonstrate a strong desire

---

[14] 2008 Bank of America Study of High Net-Worth Philanthropy

to "give back to the community" (81.2%) and to make an immediate difference (66.9%) in the world around them. Other leading motivations include these individuals' social (70.4%) and political beliefs (58.5%), as well as their loyalty to certain causes and organizations (70.7%) – many of whose missions seek to remedy an issue that may have affected the donor personally or someone close to them (57.5%). The question becomes how to you connect to the 80% that want to give back. You have to treat people differently. In fact, you might have heard in the past never to classify your supporters, but this is something you must do. Furthermore, you need to evaluate where they fall on the evolution board (follows) from one end of the spectrum which is classified as a good supporter (which is great) to the other end called a superstar (which is even better). Additional supports can be called fans and/or cheerleaders.

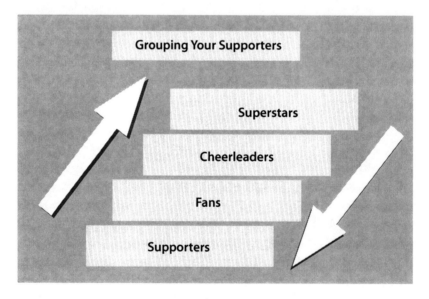

A good supporter typically comes to one of your events per year and/or donates $25 dollars when you ask and/or gives you a referral every six months. However, on the other side of the equation or top of the evolution board are Superstars. These are people who have, as one might say, "Drank the Kool-aid of your organization." They live, eat, and breathe what you do and what you're about, showing their commitment for a year or a life time. If they were a part of your basketball team they would be Lebron James or Michael Jordon. One can see their affect in results and the doors they open as well as helping in every way possible like: raising funds, introduction to major funders and sponsors, vital resources, great ideas, and emotional support of events. They often respond as my champion did at the start of this element by attending meetings with you. They're there with you, helping whether you win, lose, or draw. In many cases one superstar can equal $250,000 or more in additional funding.

You have four levels of people who can help you. They all want to help whether directly or indirectly, however the issue is their actual results. You're looking to make an investment of time and money into them, so you'll need to make sure you initially properly categorize them and then implement the right plan to foster their growth and development. Divide the group into those that can help, how much they can help, and categorize them so that you spend money, time and resources on your most important superstars.

On each end of the spectrum, you have supporters and SuperStars, but in between you have fans and cheerleaders. The key step for you to take is identifying where your investor base currently stands in relation to each level and then analyze how to either find more cheerleaders and SuperStars or persuade cheerleaders to become superstars, and fans to become cheerleaders.

As you define each category you'll need to customize it to your particular organization, keeping in mind that a fan could be someone who helps contribute $500 or more per year to your organization either in direct contribution or via their connections, while a Cheerleader is typically on the board, a volunteer, and/or key resources who provides $5,000 or more per year in funding (you'll need to set up the parameters).

Once you have identified what each group looks like in relation to your database, parameters and contacts, then you can start figuring out how to move them up the ladder and/or keep them at the superstar level. A famous saying is, "what you focus on grows," so consider adding a field in your database called support level and then categorize as appropriate.

The reality is that moving someone from Cheerleader to Superstar is easier than moving them from supporter to Superstar. You'll never know who will grow by going to the next level, but your efforts should reflect the organization's desire to strengthen your supporters. In the end, you'll have five to 10 people who will bring more value to your NPO than the other 1000 (or 10,000) combined.

You'll need to focus on the next **Element 27, Expanding Your Molecules and Increasing Your Referrals** in order to bring more SuperStars to the party.

element

27: Expand Your Molecules & Increase Referrals

"REFERRALS COME THROUGH WHO YOU ARE, NOT WHAT YOU SELL," said Bill Cates, one of the top referral gurus in the country. Bill's quote is simple but gets the point across. You'll expand your network and receive more referrals based on who you are, how well you treat others, along with the techniques you use rather than the nonprofit services you offer. You'll need to understand the power of a great 59 second commercial and the use of a tickler system to stay in touch and top of mind.

In our Fundraising Fire Course (How Good Become Great Academy,) we teach the four stages of relationship evolution; diving into strategies, techniques, and a proven process. Although for this book, we'll briefly cover some ideas to help you strengthen and expand your network. After you understand how your fundraising goals are affected by your networking strategies, you'll want to move on to tactics.

First, start changing the way you introduce yourself at networking functions. This begins with the initial part of your NPO 59 second commercial (Element 12) and then leads into a story. Most people glaze over when you start off the conversation with, "I am a Development Officer/Executive Director/VP of Development for a nonprofit that does _____ _____(fill in the blank). You can fill in any NPO description for the answer, but get the same psychological response. Try a new approach like, "I helped save 10,000 kids last year," or "we saved 500,000 trees last summer." Make the statement powerful with a pattern interrupt.

Second, take a new look at your current network. You'll need to evaluate what industries and sectors the people in your network are involved in and notice patterns. You may find that you're continuing to attend the same types of events with the same type of people. Ask yourself if it's time to branch out and try some new audiences.

Third, start evaluating the types of events you're attending. You can begin to see if you're in front of the right audiences and if the people attending these events have Connector Potential©. The events you're attending must attract people who can make a difference for you; moving mountains, and/or impacting your network. One key person with the right rolodex can expand your fundraising by $250,000 a year.

Fourth, change the way you look at leads. Your building long term relationships so ask permission to put your new contacts into your fundraising process and immediately (after helping them with a priority) ask for help. If done properly, you will receive one referral or introduction that can bring in $500,000 more per year.

It can be difficult to stay on top of referrals or asking for the right ones at the right times unless you have a good tickler system. Many people use some type of contact management database software; examples include: ACT, saleforce.com or your company's CRM system. You have your own NPO tickler system right on your computer if you use the Microsoft operating system – it is called Outlook. A tickler system enables you to flag contacts for follow up with a good system, helping you evaluate the time in between contacts and the methods used to engage the person (i.e. e-mail, phone call, letter, etc.).

Here is a level look at how an NPO tickler system works:

1. Make sure all the key people in your network are in the contacts section of outlook
2. Create a subgroup called donors and sponsors
3. Identify from your database current donor/sponsors and people you would like to invite to events or ask for specific help
4. Be sure to click on the category button and put them in the donor/sponsor category
5. Use the flag system to tickle you periodically to contact them
6. Set the flag to a date based on how you rated them
7. Briefly look at each contact and note (you can do this in several sections of the contact file) how you can help them
8. Now, after you've done something for them, utilize your 59 second NPO commercial when you reach out

The goal is to keep in touch on a basis that fits their relationship to you, their preferences, potential ability to help, and their opportunity to be a superstar for your NPO.

Your staying in touch and keeping your name top of mind for your contacts so now you want to move on to increasing the referrals and introductions you receive. Increasing referrals is easy – here is the trick or the secret – give as many referrals to other people as you possibly can, helping them to expand their network. I'll say that again, provide referrals and introductions to everyone you know as much as is humanly possible. You'll see your referrals double, triple, increase tenfold. Remember to have patience because their return gesture may take some time.

Increasing referrals is about establishing a habit and system that works for your style. Most people do not receive referrals because they simply do not ask. Bill Cates also covers using a method to let your contacts know that you desire key introductions and you want them to help you. I've identified seven key tactics you can implement to increase the number of referrals you receive:

1. *Give To Get:* Simply and continuously give your contacts referrals, value, opportunities, gifts, etc.

2. *Rewind and Remind:* Let them know as often as possible and with as many different channels as possible that you live on referrals.

3. *Testimonials:* Help the person who is going to offer the referrals to understand why they should refer you to their contact by reminding them of either the professional or personal assistance you've offered them.

4. *Create their circles:* send over a quick bullet list of "who we'd (or I) like to meet" in an e-mail message.

5. *Set the table:* Let them know how helpful it will be if they let the person know (after they've given you the name or intro) you'll be contacting them and why you'll be in touch.

6. *Details Matter:* Make sure you know all the details of the referral –who, what, where, when, how, etc.

7. *Time Counts:* Make sure you follow up immediately or within 24 hours.

Make sure as you go out and try the new techniques you avoid the 7 deadly sins of networking which are:

1. *Lack of Gratitude:* Many people fail to show their appreciation for help extended to them and overlook the fact that everyone in your network like to be appreciated. They miss opportunities to send hand-written thank you notes or value e-mails that have special meaning to their contact.

2. *Getting Before You Give:* They often try to get before they give, becoming a taker expecting help right away. They often wait to give value until the other person has made the first move or went out of their way to offer assistance.

3. *Sporadic Efforts:* Their efforts are often sporadic, attending events only during the holidays or in the summer time. Networking is a continuous process where people get to see you several times, at several functions, becoming comfortable with your style and goals.

4. *Failing the Trust Step:* They often forget to follow up or follow through on any commitments they made. Building trust is about displaying Genuine Credibility©.

5. *Providing Weak Introductions:* They rush through trying to connect people without giving the right specifics or properly setting up the rules of engagement.

6. *Mismatching People:* They are unable to articulate why two people should meet or they have such a

weak understanding of each person's strengths that they overlook connection points.

7. *Passing the Buck:* They expect others to do the work for them, passing along portfolio, services or bio information and then sitting back and waiting for the introductions to come in. They overestimate others desire and focus to help them accomplish their goals.

Increasing referrals and expanding your network comes down to the type of person you are (not what you do or say). As you continue to give to others you'll see your opportunities explode. This entire process can get easier for you if you use **Element 28, Ask for Help**.

element

28: Ask for Help

DALE CARNEGIE UNDERSTOOD THAT SIMPLE THINGS MAKE VERY big differences when he said, "If you want to gather honey, don't kick over the beehive." In fact, he understood human relationships better than most and realized that the best way to accomplish your own goals is to ask others to help you. If you do it in a professional, polite, and affectionate manner, then you'll get the help you need.

If you want people to help you, then you have to help them provide something extra, something more, and something of special value. I read Carnegie's famous book titled, "How to win friends and influence people," in high school. It has sold over 15 million copies worldwide and is a standard reading recommendation for anyone starting a business, NPO, or new process of career development. The concepts were unbelievably simple, but incredibly effective for me in the fundraising world.

I've duplicated his Top 10 list below to remind you of how interaction with potential investors and community personnel can be improved by your small changes and commitment to key actions. In fact, the slight change of calling them an investor (internally) rather than a donor can shift attitudes and in most cases, if you ask in the proper way or present yourself through the proper process, people will help you.

Top 10

1 Don't criticize, condemn or complain

2 Give honest, sincere appreciation

3 Arouse in the other person an eager want

4 Become genuinely interested in other people

5 SMILE

6 Remember that a person's name is to that person the sweetest and most important sound in any language

7 Be a good listener

8 Encourage them to talk about themselves

9 Talk in terms of the other person's interests

10 Make the other person feel important

Furthermore, you can change your NPO's culture from one of fear of fundraising to a team focused on hitting new goals and hungry for new opportunities. These changes range from the words you use to the strategies you implement. An NPO can accomplish a lot by simply having you and your staff memorize this Top 10 and begin to the harness the power of **Element 29, The Power of Duplication**.

element

29: The Power of Duplication

"OTHER PEOPLES IDEAS, EFFORTS, AND MONEY ARE THE KEY TO financial and life success," is a famous quote from Napoleon Hill's "Laws of Success" (which the Book Think and Grow Rich is the cliffs notes of). I never did forget that saying even as I read the book when I was a sophomore in College. Hill's research showed the power of duplicating your efforts. The relevance of which is not just having employees, customers or other workers, but the power of duplicating your enthusiasm, faith, and passion out in the market place.

As an NPO Officer, you have the opportunity to duplicate yourself via other people. These people help you in the community to present a similar passion, commitment, and fire. People want to get behind something important, critical, and of value. They need something bigger then themselves to believe in. You need to understand and then harness the power of duplication.

Napoleon Hill's research demonstrated the power of the Mastermind and the effects on duplicating your efforts. The Mastermind law presented the idea that when two people get together (have their minds work together) you actually create a third mind (power of thoughts) so 1+1 = 3 or 2 + 2 = 10. As you duplicate yourself through others in the community, you start to see exponential growth and opportunities. This is how you can increase from $250,000 in fundraising to $5,000,000 in three years.

Duplicating yourself in another person is similar to having someone working for you. However, in this situation you are not compensating or managing them (although you'll need to train them – we'll cover that later). Once you've duplicated your efforts out in the business community and nonprofit world, you'll receive referrals from the most un-likely sources and investment from people and firms you would have never guessed.

Strategy 6 Summary

- Define what a great relationship means to you
- Incorporate new tools for networking
- Avoid the 7 sins of networking
- Learn how to properly ask for help
- Implement methods to duplicate your efforts
- Having your entire staff memorize Dale Carnegie's Top 10 list can be very beneficial

Key Action Steps

(You Can Do This Right Now):

5. List one new idea to improve your networking

    _____

6. Divide up your current (or prospective) investor base
    – How many people do you have in each category?

    Supporters:_____   Fans: _____

    Cheerleaders:_____   SuperStars:_____

    Tool:
    *Dale Carnegie's Golden Book

*Available at HowGoodBecomeGreat.com

strategy

7. The New Back Draft

> *"Do not wait; the time will never be "just right." Start where you stand, and work with whatever tools you may have at your command, and better tools will be found as you go along.."*
>
> — Napoleon Hill

YOU CAN OFFER PROFESSIONALLY ESTABLISHED SPONSOR PACKages and offerings. Every industry has improved and Sponsorship formatting is no exception to this rule. Although this book is not about technology or new web applications, you must have a feel for the tools that can help your fundraising efforts. Understand how marketing and sales tools work to increase your fundraising efforts, including proper ways to implement and which tools are necessary versus which ones are nice to haves. As you learn more about the Fundraising Formula you'll start to ignite a Blazing Fundraising Fire.

30:
New
Strategies for
Sponsorships

"ON THE BRIGHT SIDE, THE RECOVERY NOW IS SHOWING SIGNS of life. Conversations with buyers and sellers reflect optimism, and so we predict the $100 million and more will come back into the market in 2010 as the recession fades in the rearview mirror and corporate budgetary restrictions are relaxed." This quote is from Sponsorship.com and reflects the state of national sponsorship statistics. The reality is that multimillion dollar for-profit firms continue to sponsor all kinds of local nonprofit & community events, professional athletes and sports teams, well-known musicians/bands, and other unique properties, assets, and opportunities. This is still a significant component of the overall marketing, sales, and promotions strategies for most firms (both large and small) even though the recession has slowed down the overall spending. Why aren't they sponsoring your NPO?

The number one mistake that most nonprofits make is approaching all potential sponsors with a one-size-fits-all offer. You need a new strategy to grow the quantity and improve the quality of the sponsors you currently sign on. If you obtain a better understanding of their current challenges, of what potential sponsors require, of how the game has changed, and of the proper way to implement new tactics, then you'll start to hit increased sponsorship revenue goals.

There are four generic reasons why firms sponsor and then 100's of hidden expectations under those reasons. These overarching reasons include:

- Firms diversify their advertising budget & gain approval of customers and key stakeholders
- Firms respond to consumer-changing social attitudes
- Firms target efforts in certain geographical areas (local communities)
- Firms enhance brand equity through image and awareness

One of the major challenges with launching a successful sponsorship program, whether it is for an event or for your NPO directly, is the lack of research data regarding results and success and/or failure of sponsorships in general. It quickly becomes difficult to identify what has worked in the past and what could be failing now. Many NPO events and organizations are sponsored by the business community because those firms want to help the local citizens and their client base following the reasons mentioned above. However, identifying their ROI can be difficult if not impossible. Your frustration can grow when you ask them why they sponsor specific events and their answers are often vague or non objective such as, "Well,

Henry plays golf with Sue," or "their kids go to school to-gether." These types of answers demonstrate the difficulty in cutting through the shallow, superficial reasons to get to the business objectives and potentially help them identify objective reasons for engagement.

Each firm that you approach is weighted down by too many opportunities with too little cash. They're challenged to make good decisions and investments that have a return on investment and of course, make everyone involved feel good. They need you to help them make a good decision, which often requires you to tell them that your NPO is not a good fit for their sponsorship dollar. They need a consultant, not an NPO well wisher, because they struggle to quantify the results from analyzing potential sponsorship opportunities. In fact, they often make important decisions with only half the correct information or based on past habits (we've always sponsored ABC event).

Many NPOs add to this problem by only using the philanthropy angle. They assume that the local large and medium sized corporations will help because they want to give back and end up bunched in with all the 100's of local agencies with their hand out asking for the same type of relationship. All nonprofits are helping people, animals, and issues that need to be addressed, providing significant care and impact, but for-profit corporations see the world through black and white glasses and need additional business reasons to participate. The emotional pulling on the heart strings is a great tactic, but overused. Your organization ends up blending in with all the rest and instead of becoming the pink cat (Strategy 3) you're just another cat (with the same cry).

In other words, your event looks like just another rubber chicken dinner or another creative attempt to offer a different type of handball game. They will sponsor your organization if you act different and present objective, customized data that helps them make a great decision.

You need the right information at your finger tips and the right questions in order to provide the value that sponsors are looking for and this starts with your own NPO goals. Here are five key questions to ask at this point:

- What value do you offer the potential sponsor?
- What impact can you have on their business?
- What is the NPOs overall goal of the sponsorship (why do you need it)?
- What is your story or 59 second commercial?
- What could corporate support mean to your NPO?

Once you understand your goals and WIFT (What is in it for them), you can begin to identify a few mistakes you may be making with regard to approaching sponsors. Many NPOs try to emulate the same approach that very large, successful for-profits use. For example, naming rights continues to be a heavily used tool. The naming rights benefit works for you sponsor, but you need to implement this offer differently than the way NASCAR or PGA sponsors use this feature. You want to watch the positive tactics they use and filter out the problem areas (out of reach budget tactics). Frankly, most NPOs spend too much money on fancy brochures and marketing material overlooking the importance of offering great value at a low sponsorship fee. They end up spending a significant portion on their budget using a shot gun approach with results coming in on a hit or miss basis. They overlook the importance of targeting the right prospects, building a case for why their event or NPO is a perfect fit, and then ending up with no budget for sponsorship sales tactics.

According to IEG[15], most sponsors desire interaction on the ROI level, including more timely updates, new tools to gather data, and a closer relationship to the sponsor. If you hear the word "No" from a sponsor it could mean you've made one of a few mistakes. First, you should not have been talking to them in the first place because they were not a fit. Perhaps they don't work with your type of event or organization or they lack the necessary budget, or they don't sponsor events at all. In this case, they were not your ideal target. Second, you did not demonstrate the objective tools you will use to provide them feedback. For example, they want names and mailing addresses and you'll give them logo location all over the place. Third, you don't have an ongoing communication strategy with them so the potential sponsor cannot create long term connection points. For example, if you only talk to your event guests a month before the event and then do not communicate for a year, then the sponsor will have difficulty communicating with these prospective customers on an ongoing base as well.

Obtaining more new sponsors and keeping the existing ones is more about improving your sales techniques and processes and less about great brochures, web sites and creative ideas. You need a system and process that initially gets you in front of the right firms with the right decision makers and then helps you lead them to the best option for their business. Now is the time to change the way you offer sponsorships and watch your events explode. You need to shift your focus to the tactics laid out in **Element 31, Professional Sponsorship Selling**.

---

[15] www.sponsorship.com

element

31: Professional Sponsorship Selling

"OUR GOAL IS TO GO UP BY 12% IN NET AT THE EVENT." OUR EVENT chair said at a recent meeting. He was articulating that in a down economy we're increasing sponsorship amounts and volume. Why? Denver Active 20-30 has figured out the game over the years and the number one key is selling sponsorships (Real, identifiable ROI), not asking for just a donation. We've shifted the culture from one of begging (Borrower Phenomenon) to one of offering professional sponsorships (value exceeding the sponsor dollar).

In this chapter, I'll briefly discuss some techniques and tools for identifying potential sponsors, engaging them, and having them sign their sponsor form. I've divided this subject into two areas; event sponsorship and NPO sponsorship. This process helps NPO Officers understand why firms are not sponsoring NPO events (or at least not your event). Once you understand the problems we can cover solutions.

There are several reasons why the businesses in your local community are not investing in (sponsoring) your event or your organization. Typically you have not shown them value in the following areas:

- Positive Publicity
- Generated New Sales
- Enhanced Image
- Expanded client base
- Reached new markets

When it comes to event sponsorship, the best way to start offering professional sponsorships is follow the fundraising formula (CQ+P³ = Funds) for your day to day activities and then focus on the DRAFT Process. This process involves five steps where D stands for Display and includes the "look and feel" of the event or your group. You already know that your event and everything connected to it has to look professional (All collateral -web site, material, e-mail, packages, location), but all of this must be done within an expected budget (most of this can be done in-kind trade). There is a fine line between spending too much and too little.

Next, R stands for results. You must tie the event to the investors expected results and help them articulate and define what success will or will not look like, hence, the objective reasons to help them come back next year. The key question here is, "How will you know your sponsorship has been successful?"

The third part is A and stands for angle. This deals with how you position your event and demands that you take a look at competitive factors including when you schedule it, other and similar events going on, time of year, and potential sponsor stealers (i.e. your sponsor's perception of other events being bigger, better, stronger than yours).

The F stands for Feedback and requires you to get feedback not only after the event and throughout the year, but during it. If something isn't working during the event whether it is a 75 minute breakfast or all day affair, make the change right then and there if the sponsor wants it.

The last part is T or Track and involves ongoing communication and opportunities throughout the year. Promote your sponsors at every event, each media opportunity, and keep the lines of communication open (stay in touch and offer value). Make sure they have access to the event guests if that is their preference.

There are many organizations overlooking opportunities to create investment chances for firms and people in their local community that go beyond just events. Similar to the for-profit world, you can offer naming rights, logo combo products and services, and many other great ideas. The same rules apply as mentioned in the DRAFT process, but the key is to engage them at a deeper level and offer a closer connection, often to your client base (the people or animals you serve), continuing to ask important questions, customizing your solutions, and paying attention to their concerns and fears (not yours). As you improve the professionalism of your sponsor offerings, you can look to **Element 32, Leveraging WEB 2.0**.

element

32: Leveraging WEB 2.0

"NOW IS THE TIME TO HARNESS THE POWER OF WEB 2.0," THE teleseminar leader said during his call. This was a few months before our Webplicity 2.0 book would come out. My co-author and I had realized that we had to cover the new interactive world of social media, search, and user-driven content. It was becoming too big to ignore. We wrote the book targeting for-profit businesses; however, the greatest opportunity could be in the NPO world. The challenge is that it can be difficult for NPO Officers to understand what it means let alone try to figure out how to harness this power. There are plenty of books and experts on this subject so I'll simply touch on it from a fundraising strategy point of view.

You hear a lot of buzz and conversation about Web 2.0 these days. The term is commonly associated with web applications that facilitate interactive information sharing, user-centered content and often called the second generation of the World Wide Web. It is a category of technologies created for people who use media; accessing the web as active contributors, customizing their own experience for their own reasons.

The first step is to understand what tools are considered part of the web 2.0 tool box. These include RSS, blogs, social web sites and applications, and webinars. RSS stands for Really Simple Syndication and is a way of showing content (news, pics, audio files) without having to go to different web sites to get the content. For example, if you use a major new site like Fox News or CNN, then you can use an RSS feed to have your content aggregated or receive only the information you're interested in.

We've all had experience by now with social media. You've probably visited a blog and you (or your NPO) have a Face Book or LinkedIn account. In fact, you might use some type of YouTube or MySpace application. These are all tools meant to help the user of the web gain more value and save time. Are you utilizing these technologies to the benefit of your fundraising efforts?

Development and key Officers often overlook the importance of both their personal and organization's social media tools. It can become overwhelming very quickly so just focus on a few key points. First, make it part of your overall development plan. Second, understand how each platform is different and what works and what does not with each (i.e. twitter vs. Face Book, etc.). Third, experiment with it. Finally, here are four key tools your organization must use:

1. Event Face Book Page
2. Officer LinkedIn profile (Event ROI)
3. Event YouTube video of event (MP3 file(s) as well)
4. Officer Blog (describing the sponsor ROI)

The last part of Web 2.0 includes tools like webinars, online training/meetings, and audio seminars and tools. You can take advantage of these tools by beginning to utilize them for fundraising prospecting activities. In my academy I show you how to use the tools to effectively target, prospect, and close more key investors (major sponsors and donors).

In the next **Element 33, Social Media Research**, I discuss social media training sources and some tricks and secrets. Again, there are plenty of experts on this subject, but I'd like to help you leverage the tools into your NPO fundraising strategies.

element

33: Social Media Research

"OVER 230 MILLION FACE BOOK ACCOUNTS ARE ACTIVE," THE trainer yelled out at a recent workshop." As I took this number in I started to wonder how many nonprofits are struggling with which tools to focus on let alone what types of content and strategies to use to take advantage of this new media.

Social media is a term that describes the conversation and interaction between people online. The word "media" in this case does not notate the traditional meaning, rather it means digital words, sounds, and content shared among users on the web producing cultural, social or financial (donations/sponsorships) value. The tools are used to spread or circulate through social interaction. In other words, the audience watching the movie participates in deciding the plot, surprises, and ending.

Most businesses and even less nonprofits are taking advantage of the new channels and tools. However, there are several sources for your research that can help bring you up to speed and help your personal fundraising efforts. These include:

Collaboration Tools:

Social News – Mixx, Digg, NowPublic

Social Bookmarking/tagging – Google Readers, StumbleUpon

Wikis – Wikimedia, Wetpaint

Messaging:

Blogs – Blogger.com, TypePad

Events – Meetup, eventful, upcoming

Micro-blogging – Jaiku, twitter, tumblr, Qaiku, Yammer

Social Networking – LinkedIn, Facebook, geni.com, hi5, MySpace, Ning, orkut, qzone, skyrock, renren, kaixin, xing, and about 50 others

Multimedia:

Audio Sharing – MySpace, ccmixter, sharethemusic

Livecasting – ustream.tv, Skype, openCU

Presentation – Slideshare, brainshark

Reviews:

Business Reviews – customer lobby

Community – Yahoo! Answers, Wiki answers, Google Answers

Product reviews - Epinion.com

Aggregators:

Twine, Netvibes

I spend 1/2 of one of the academy classes (I have a social media expert lead this) reviewing and focusing on strategies for utilizing these tools. This helps the NPO leader understand, articulate, and implement the right plan to help their organization use new channels to hit new fundraising levels. You too, can incorporate a social media plan into your investor development plan.

element

Throw Fuel On It To Ignite a Blazing Fund-raising Fire

34:

""YOUR LIFE, YOUR BUSINESS, YOUR JOY IS WHAT YOU THINK IT IS, your dreams come from within, and your results are decided ahead of time. This all happens inside your own head before you take the first step."

This is my quote and I live it each day. If you want to become a better fundraiser, then it starts with your individual ability and activities. You determine your results before you start, which can be great, if you follow the five steps in the Fundraising Formula.

The Formula was established for simplicity and a chronological guide to make your life easier.

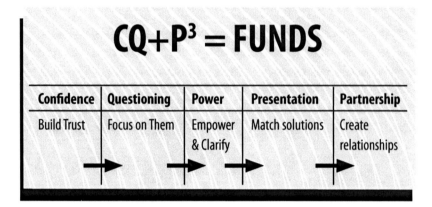

$CQ+P^3 = FUNDS$

Confidence	Questioning	Power	Presentation	Partnership
Build Trust	Focus on Them	Empower & Clarify	Match solutions	Create relationships

The process is about improvement over perfection and focuses you on small shifts keeping in mind the value you bring to the NPO world.

Cheat Sheet -

C = Your Confidence increases the confidence your prospective investor has in you (We do business with people we like and trust)

Q = Questioning to learn about their concerns, opportunities, challenges (focus on them)

P^3

P = POWER means understanding both the decision maker and how to harness the POWER of your Board, Volunteers and Community

P^2 = Presentation means to match your solutions and offerings (benefits your NPO produces) with the challenges of your investor

P^3 = Partnership means creating great long term partnerships with staff, clients, investors, volunteers, board directors, and in-kind vendors

You must evaluate the details of what is being asked of you and if you understand your clients, employees, and Boards expectations. If you do, then you can start to improve your own skills and knowledge, elevating your own individual contributions. Lastly, the NPO you represent is looking for you to offer more in the way of collaboration, knowledge, processes, and relationships but they can't always articulate their needs or how to put you on the path to production and reaching those goals. Great training can do this.

Summary

KEY LEARNING POINTS:

- Understand the new ways to sell sponsorships
- Professional Sponsor selling is more about the prospects perception of your process then the event
- Cleary define Web 2.0 for your NPO
- Pick up some great research sites/links to improve your understanding of social media
- Understand your technology choices

Key Action Steps

(You Can Do This Right Now):

7. List one new way to improve your sponsorship sales

    _____

8. Which part of the Fundraising Formula will cause
    you the largest challenge?

C _____   Q _____   POWER: _____

Presentation: _____   Partnership: _____

Tool:
***Sign up for Fundraising Fire Course**

Available at HowGoodBecomeGreat.com

How Good
Become Great
Academy

Web Site **www.HowGoodBecomeGreat.com** or
www.BillYounginspires.com

- Lots of great tips and articles
- FREE Stuff
- Interactive Blog
- Sign up for the e-mail newsletter
- Register for a webinar or workshop
- Ask questions
- Follow us on twitter or connect on face book

Webinars & Workshops

How Good Board Members Become Great Fundraisers (Initial 60 minute webinar that expands on the book plus quarterly How Good Become Great webinar trainings for board members and volunteers)

Ignite a Blazing Fundraising Fire

Talus Tuesdays

Young Success (Focused on young entrepreneurs)

Other books

<u>How Good Board Members Become Great Fundraisers, Overcoming the 7 Critical Challenges Volunteers Face</u> (available at billyounginspires.com)

<u>Webplicity</u> (Available at amazon.com or bn.com)

<u>Webplicity 2.0</u> (Available at amazon.com or bn.com)

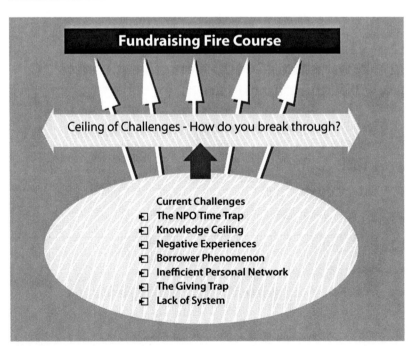

Academy

There are very few hands on, real world training courses in the country for improving your fundraising efforts. This course is unique in the industry, created for executive directors, development officers, entrepreneurs, and anyone involved in the fundraising game. Attendees can expect to learn more about fundraising in eight weeks than they have their entire life. Lastly, the tools mentioned in this book are available at the Academy or at the web site (Note: some tools are provided for free while others incorporate a fee) and include:

- SuperStars Tool
- BURN Assessment
- Goal Card
- Gratitude Form
- Tickler System
- Contribution Tracker
- SPARK Drill
- And many others

In this eight-week webinar/workshop you and your key team and volunteer members will learn how to:

- Develop and maintain relationships
- Ask the right questions to identify ideal donors
- Discern what motivates people and companies to give
- Broaden your network & ask for referrals
- Explode your fundraising levels

Thank You

Thank you to Francies Gibbs my darling Grandmother and one of the reasons I've lived such a great life. She gave me this poem when I went away to College – The Man in the Glass. Thanks Grandma.

When you get what you want in your struggle for self,
And the world makes you King for a day,
Then go to the mirror and look at yourself,
And see what that guy (person) has to say.

For it isn't your Father, or Mother, or Wife, or Husband whose judgment upon you must pass. The person whose verdict counts most in your life Is the person staring back from the glass.

They are the person to please, never mind all the rest, For their with you clear up to the end, And you've passed your most dangerous, difficult test If the person in the glass is your friend.

You may be like Jack Horner and "chisel" a plum,
And think you're a wonderful person, But the person in the glass says you're only a bum If you can't look them straight in the eye.

You can fool the whole world down the pathway of years, And get pats on the back as you pass, But your final reward will be heartaches and tears If you've cheated the person in the glass.

Dale Wimbrow, The Guy in the Glass

CPSIA information can be obtained at www.ICGtesting.com
Printed in the USA
BVOW061553160512

290314BV00001B/49/P